Mapping the Risks

Assessing the Homeland Security Implications of Publicly Available Geospatial Information

JOHN C. BAKER, BETH E. LACHMAN, DAVID R. FRELINGER, KEVIN M. O'CONNELL, ALEXANDER C. HOU, MICHAEL S. TSENG, DAVID ORLETSKY, CHARLES YOST

Prepared for the National Geospatial-Intelligence Agency
Approved for public release, distribution unlimited

 NATIONAL DEFENSE RESEARCH INSTITUTE

The research described in this report was prepared for the National Geospatial-Intelligence Agency. The research was conducted in the RAND National Defense Research Institute, a federally funded research and development center supported by the Office of the Secretary of Defense, the Joint Staff, the unified commands, and the defense agencies under Contract DASW01-01-C-0004.

Library of Congress Cataloging-in-Publication Data

Mapping the risks : assessing homeland security implications of publicly available geospatial information / John C. Baker ... [et al.].
    p. cm.
    "MG-142."
    Includes bibliographical references.
    ISBN 0-8330-3547-9 (pbk. : alk. paper)
    1. Civil defense—United States. 2. Geographic information systems—Defense measures—United States. I. Baker, John C., 1949–

UA927.M26 2004
363.34'7'0285—dc22

                                      2003027797

The RAND Corporation is a nonprofit research organization providing objective analysis and effective solutions that address the challenges facing the public and private sectors around the world. RAND's publications do not necessarily reflect the opinions of its research clients and sponsors.

RAND® is a registered trademark.

Published 2004 by the RAND Corporation
1700 Main Street, P.O. Box 2138, Santa Monica, CA 90407-2138
1200 South Hayes Street, Arlington, VA 22202-5050
201 North Craig Street, Suite 202, Pittsburgh, PA 15213-1516
RAND URL: http://www.rand.org/
To order RAND documents or to obtain additional information, contact
Distribution Services: Telephone: (310) 451-7002;
Fax: (310) 451-6915; Email: order@rand.org

Preface

This report assesses the homeland security implications of publicly available geospatial data and information. Specifically, it seeks to frame the analytical issues concerning whether and how this type of data and information that is available from U.S. government sources can be exploited by terrorists and other adversaries seeking to attack U.S. critical infrastructure and other key homeland locations. We give particular attention to surveying and characterizing these federal data and information within the broader context of diverse public- and private-sector producers of potentially relevant geospatial information.

The analysis presented in this report should be of interest to U.S. government decisionmakers and analysts concerned with homeland security, geospatial information, and the security risks that could arise from publicly accessible information. This report presents a framework for analysis that could be helpful to U.S. federal government decisionmakers responsible for developing and revising agency data policies that concern public access to geospatial data and information sources. Although the report mainly focuses on federal geospatial information sources, the analytical framework could be relevant to other decisionmakers and analysts at the state and local government levels, and those in the private sector, who deal with similar issues.

As noted in the following memorandum for the record, this research was undertaken for the National Geospatial-Intelligence

Agency (NGA, formerly the National Imagery and Mapping Agency). The U.S. Geological Survey (USGS) of the Department of the Interior served as NGA's study partner. The research was conducted within the Intelligence Policy Center of the RAND National Defense Research Institute, a federally funded research and development center sponsored by the Office of the Secretary of Defense, the Joint Staff, the unified commands, and the defense agencies.

Sponsor Guidance

NATIONAL IMAGERY AND MAPPING AGENCY
4600 SANGAMORE ROAD
BETHESDA, MARYLAND 20816-5003

U-061-03/PAM   27 June 2003

MEMORANDUM FOR RECORD

SUBJECT: RAND vulnerability report

1. Following the events of September 11, 2001, the National
Imagery and Mapping Agency (NIMA) substantially increased its
support to federal, state and local entities involved in
homeland security and defense. Our expanded involvement in
providing unclassified domestic geospatial data and analytic
services to a broad community caused us to consider whether
public availability of geospatial information on our major
cities and infrastructures increased vulnerability to terrorist
attack.

2. NIMA asked the RAND Corporation to develop a framework to
assist us, and others, in assessing these potential risks. This
report is intended to provide that initial framework, and to
guide public and private decision makers in weighing homeland
security implications related to release of geospatial
information. The report describes three analytic filters that
can assist decision makers in systematically assessing the
vulnerabilities of geospatial data. It is a point of departure
for the elaboration of operational guidelines to address this
important issue.

Anita I. Cohen

ANITA I. COHEN
Director, Office of Americas
National Imagery and Mapping Agency

The RAND Corporation Quality Assurance Process

Peer review is an integral part of all RAND research projects. Prior to publication, this document, as with all documents in the RAND monograph series, was subject to a quality assurance process to ensure that the research meets several standards, including the following: The problem is well formulated; the research approach is well designed and well executed; the data and assumptions are sound; the findings are useful and advance knowledge; the implications and recommendations follow logically from the findings and are explained thoroughly; the documentation is accurate, understandable, cogent, and temperate in tone; the research demonstrates understanding of related previous studies; and the research is relevant, objective, independent, and balanced. Peer review is conducted by research professionals who were not members of the project team.

RAND routinely reviews and refines its quality assurance process and also conducts periodic external and internal reviews of the quality of its body of work. For additional details regarding the RAND quality assurance process, visit http://www.rand.org/standards/.

Contents

Figures

Tables

Summary

In the wake of the September 11, 2001 terrorist attacks, U.S. officials have instituted information protection policies aimed at bolstering homeland security. These policies aim to minimize the opportunities of potential attackers exploiting publicly available information they might obtain from federal sources in planning attacks against U.S. homeland locations.

Of particular concern to U.S. officials are the federal sources of geospatial information. Geospatial data and information are useful for identifying various geographical features of U.S. locations and facilities, as well as characterizing their important attributes. Although federal agencies produce and publicly disseminate such information for a wide range of beneficial purposes, the risk also exists that some types of geospatial information could be exploited by terrorists. Federal agencies thus face a challenge in deciding which types of geospatial information should be publicly accessible, as well as whether and how to restrict new sensitive information as it becomes available.

Study Purpose and Approach

This study frames the analytical issues associated with assessing whether and how geospatial data and information that is publicly available from U.S. federal agencies can be exploited by potential attackers, including terrorists, for attacking U.S. critical infrastructure and other key homeland locations. The results of our analysis yield insights that can assist federal and other decisionmakers by high-lighting key factors they should consider in addressing this issue. The study also offers an analytical process that can serve as an initial framework for assessing publicly available geospatial information in order to understand its homeland security implications.

The Need for a Framework to Support Decisionmaking

Decisionmakers are faced with the task of deciding whether publicly accessible geospatial information poses a risk to protecting critical infrastructure and, if so, whether to restrict public access to the information. After September 11, officials had to make decisions about restricting such access under conditions of time pressures and without much top-level guidance. However, even under the best circumstances, assessing what information is potentially sensitive and what warrants restriction is not easy. An analytical process can assist decisionmakers by

- providing a structured and consistent approach to identifying sensitive geospatial information
- ensuring that all relevant factors are weighed
- providing an explicit methodology and rationale to justify and explain the decision.

A basic premise of our analysis is, therefore, that sound decisions about the security benefits of restricting a particular piece or type of geospatial information depend on considering their homeland security implications in broader contexts. These implications are the following:

- *Usefulness*: the potential usefulness of geospatial information for planning attacks on critical U.S. sites. Attackers require particular kinds of information to identify targets and plan attacks.
- *Uniqueness*: the uniqueness of federal geospatial information sources. If alternative sources of the same information are readily available, the net security benefits of restricting access to the information may be minimal or nonexistent.

- *Benefits and Costs*: the expected societal benefits and costs of restricting the information. The chief benefit of restricting public access to geospatial information should be to improve U.S. homeland security against an attack. However, any expected benefits also must be weighed against expected societal costs, which are likely to exist because of the many important public- and private-sector uses.

A "Supply" and "Demand" Approach to Developing the Framework

To help decisionmakers think about these broader contexts, we conducted analysis intended to derive a framework for factoring these considerations into decisions about whether to restrict public access to geospatial information. We used a two-pronged approach to formulate this framework:

- We assessed attackers' potential information needs—the "demand."
- We thoroughly examined federal sources of publicly available geospatial information—the "supply"—and reviewed a sampling of alternative nonfederal sources that provide similar types of information.

Scope of the Analysis

We defined geospatial information broadly, including geospatial data and information that exist in a variety of forms and are accessible through various media and sources. The forms range from raw geospatial data (e.g., latitude and longitude coordinates, maps and nautical charts, aerial and satellite images, textual geospatial descriptions) to relatively sophisticated geospatial datasets (e.g., detailed, high-accuracy geographic information system [GIS] databases).

Because of tasking and time constraints, this study does not address the following related topics, which fall outside the scope of this report:

- information without a direct or indirect geospatial characteristic

- data and information that are classified or withheld from the public under the Freedom of Information Act for homeland security or national security purposes
- new and potentially sensitive information that might be created via the integration of data from diverse sources
- nonsecurity rationales for restricting public access to data.

Demand: Assessing Attackers' Information Requirements

Methodology
To gain insights on the key information needs of potential attackers on the U.S. homeland, we undertook an analysis involving a series of postulated attacks on a spectrum of critical infrastructure, military targets, and cultural and social targets. The rationales for the attacks were derived from plausible attacker motivations, historic preferences for attack modalities by a number of real-world organizations, opportunities associated with some weapon systems that are becoming more widespread, and the use of modern techniques and tools for targeting (e.g., remote sensing, geospatial information systems, GPS [Global Positioning System], range finders). These attacks were quantitatively evaluated in terms of the likely damage they would cause. The results of these assessments informed our analysis and the findings presented in this report.

Analysis
Attackers can take advantage of the relatively accessible nature of the United States, where a substantial number of critical infrastructure facilities (e.g., airports, tunnels) and other key locations are publicly accessible or can be directly observed from a distance. Attackers can choose opportunistically among a broad range of U.S. homeland locations, different strategic objectives and related targeting objectives, and a variety of attack modes ranging from ground attacks with explosives to standoff weapon systems and area weapons (e.g., chemical, radiological). Attackers also have flexibility in both choosing

among potential targets and the information they use in planning and undertaking an attack.

The geospatial information requirements of potential attackers fall largely into two categories:

- information for *selecting a target* (i.e., Which target?, Where is it located?)
- information for *planning the attack* (i.e., What is the target's layout, vulnerabilities, security measures, etc.?).

The first type of information assists attackers in identifying a potential target and determining its general location. The attacker benefits from today's "information abundance"—that is, both geospatial and nongeospatial information is widely available from many sources. In comparison, planning an assault requires detailed and timely information for the attacker to have confidence in executing a successful operation against a given target. This planning can require information on the internal features of the selected target site (e.g., control centers, power sources), the potential vulnerabilities of the facility, and a facility's current security practices. In these cases, attackers confront a situation of relative "information scarcity" in terms of what is publicly available.

Findings

In terms of the information demands of potential attackers, our key findings are as follows:

- **Attackers have substantial flexibility in fulfilling their information needs for attacking U.S. homeland locations.** In principle, this flexibility includes a broad range of choices about why, where, and how attacks will be made. This has important implications for the types of information that attackers need and can acquire for target selection and attack planning. Our assessment of attackers' information requirements suggests that, given this degree of flexibility, publicly accessible geospatial information is probably not the first choice for fulfilling these needs. Publicly accessible geospatial information has the potential to be somewhat useful for helping with selecting a target and determining its location. However, potential attackers, such as terrorist groups or hostile governments, are more likely to desire more reliable and timely information, which is often obtainable via other means, such as through direct access or observation. In addition, many types of attacks, such as those by ground parties, are likely to require detailed information for attack planning purposes (depending on the target type and mode of attack). This type of information, which mostly comes from such nongeospatial sources as engineering textbooks or human expertise on the operations of a particular type of industrial complex, is essential for attackers to have a high confidence in their plan.

- **Opportunistic attackers, such as terrorists, usually possess the advantage of having access to diverse sources for meeting their mission-critical information needs, as well as the freedom to adjust the attack to meet the amount of information available.** An important distinction exists between what is critical information for the attacker (i.e., information with which the terrorist could not perform the attack), what is useful (but was not necessary to undertake the attack), and what is other nonessential information. Lacking critical information on a target could in theory discourage an attacker from proceeding with a given attack. In practice, however, an opportunistic attacker, such as a terrorist group, can exploit diverse information sources (ranging from direct observation to publicly available geospatial information) to meet critical information needs, while the defender faces the challenge of denying the attacker access to all relevant sources of information. The attacker can also change the mode of attack to better match the amount and type of information available. For example, if information is unavailable to support a direct assault on a target, standoff attacks on a different part of the complex or attacks outside the most heavily defended area producing the same or similar effect could be substituted. Similarly, if detailed plans are unavailable on a target to facilitate the use of precisely placed munitions, weapons with a larger area of impact or different phenomenology might be used to generate the desired impact.

Supply: Assessing the Significance of Publicly Available Geospatial Information

Methodology

Our supply analysis focused on two key questions: (1) What federal geospatial information is publicly available? and (2) How significant is it to attackers' needs given the usefulness and uniqueness of the information? Namely, significance is a combined measure of *usefulness* and *uniqueness*. For this analysis, we identified and examined geospatial data using three main methods:

- **Identifying federal geospatial information sources.** We conducted a structured survey to identify and assess publicly available geospatial information about critical sites at 465 federal data sources. This systematic search involved several person-months of effort and the searching of more than 5,000 federal Web sites to identify and examine federal activities that provide publicly accessible geospatial information. We supplemented this search with selected interviews and hard-copy document reviews.
- **Sampling of geospatial datasets from federal sources.** Once federal sources for publicly available geospatial information were identified, we examined particular sources in more detail to determine whether they contained information that might be relevant to a potential attacker's information needs. Of these sources, we identified a selected sample of 629 federal datasets[1]

---

[1] A dataset refers to a single data file, Web page, or document containing geospatial information, while a database refers to an organized collection of datasets—that is, a set of data files. An example of a database is the National Atlas of the United States (see www.

that looked like they might contain some type of geospatially oriented critical-site information. We chose this sample by identifying datasets that appeared most likely to contain sensitive geospatial information about U.S. critical sites.

- **A sampling of alternative geospatial information sources.** Since our primary focus was on federal sources, we conducted a similar, though less thorough, systematic survey to identify and sample nonfederal sources (e.g., private-sector organizations, state and local governments, academic institutions, nongovernmental organizations [NGOs], foreign sources). This involved searching more than 2,000 nonfederal Web sites to identify and examine nonfederal activities that provide publicly accessible geospatial information and the identification of a sample of more than 300 nonfederal alternative sources. This search was not meant to be exhaustive; rather, we sought to selectively sample alternatives to understand the range of other sources and identify and examine ones that most likely contained sensitive geospatial information about U.S. critical sites.

Analysis

To assess the significance of federal geospatial information to an attacker's information needs, we performed three steps for our sample of 629 federal datasets:

1. Using our "demand" analysis, we assessed and ranked the usefulness of each federal geospatial dataset to the attacker's information needs.
2. We assessed and ranked the availability of the same or similar geospatial information from alternative sources to determine the uniqueness of each federal geospatial dataset.
3. We assessed and ranked the significance of the federal geospatial information by combining the measures of usefulness and uniqueness. This combination is important because a dataset

---

nationalatlas.gov), which contains population, water, species, land cover, boundary files, and many other datasets.

that is both useful and unique would be considered more sensitive information and parts of the dataset may warrant restriction.

Findings

Our findings concerning the supply of publicly available geospatial information from federal agencies and other sources are as follows:

- **Our federal geospatial information survey found that publicly available geospatial information is spread across a wide range of federal government agencies and offices.** Many different agencies serve as major distributors of publicly available geospatial information. We identified 465 programs, offices, or major initiatives at 30 different federal agencies and departments that make various types of geospatial information publicly accessible.
- **Our analysis found that very few of the publicly accessible federal geospatial sources appear useful to meeting a potential attacker's information needs.** Fewer than 6 percent of the 629 federal geospatial information datasets we examined appeared as though they could be useful to a potential attacker. Further, we found no publicly available federal geospatial datasets that we considered critical to meeting the attacker's information needs (i.e., those that the attacker could not perform the attack without).
- **Our analysis suggests that most publicly accessible federal geospatial information is unlikely to provide significant (i.e., useful and unique) information for satisfying attackers' information needs.** Fewer than 1 percent of the 629 federal datasets we examined appeared both potentially useful and unique. Moreover, since the September 11 attacks, these information sources are no longer being made public by federal agencies.[2] However, we cannot conclude that *publicly accessible* federal geospatial

---

[2] These federal geospatial sources have either been completely withdrawn from public access on the World Wide Web, or their agencies have implemented password protection to control access.

information provides no special benefit to the attacker. Neither can we conclude that it would benefit the attacker. Our sample suggests that the information, if it exists, is not distributed widely and may be scarce.

- **In many cases, diverse alternative geospatial and nongeospatial information sources exist for meeting the information needs of potential attackers.** In our sampling of more than 300 publicly available nonfederal geospatial information alternative sources, we found that the same, similar, or more useful geospatial information on U.S. critical sites is available from a diverse set of nonfederal sources. These sources include industry and commercial businesses, academic institutions, NGOs, state and local governments, international sources, and even private citizens who publish relevant materials on the World Wide Web. Some geospatial data and information that these nonfederal sources distribute are derived from federal sources that are publicly accessible. Similarly, these nonfederal organizations are increasingly becoming sources of geospatial data and information for various federal agencies (see Chapter Three for additional discussion). In addition, relevant information is often obtainable via direct access or direct observation of the U.S. critical site.

Framework to Support Decisionmaking

Our demand and supply analysis, along with a corresponding analysis of the broader societal benefits and costs of public access to geospatial information, identified key factors relevant to assessing the homeland security implications of geospatial information. Drawing on these insights, this study suggests that a useful, first-step framework for assessing geospatial information should incorporate at least three key factors: the usefulness of the information to an attacker, the uniqueness of the information, and the societal benefits and costs of restricting public access to a particular geospatial information source (see Table S.1). These factors, or "filters," offer decisionmakers and

Table S.1
Top-Level Framework for Analysis of the Homeland Security Sensitivity of
Geospatial Data and Information Sources

Filter	Key Questions
Usefulness	Is the information useful for target selection or location purposes?
	Is the information useful for attack planning purposes?
Uniqueness	Is the information readily available from other geospatial information sources?
	Is the information available from direct observation or other information types?
Societal benefits and costs	What are the expected security benefits of restricting public access to the source?
	What are the expected societal costs of restricting public access to the source?

analysts a more structured method for assessing the sensitivity of geo-spatial information. For individual geospatial datasets, federal deci-sionmakers could use this framework to help assess whether to restrict access to part or all of the database. In addition, this framework is relevant to all distributors of geospatial information, including indus-try, state and local governments, NGOs, and academic institutions. How would decisionmakers apply this framework? Decisionmakers would ask pertinent questions for each filter. The filtering questions would then be applied sequentially. To begin, decisionmakers would evaluate a particular piece of geospatial information through the first filter by asking whether the information could be useful for either the target selection or location, or the attack planning purposes of a potential attacker. Next, the information would be subject to the sec-ond filter, which focuses on assessing whether the information is rela-tively unique—that is, whether the geospatial information in question could be readily obtained by potential attackers using other sources. These sources could be either nonfederal geospatial (e.g., private-sector or state or local sources) or from direct access to or observation of a potential target without incurring significant risks of being caught. Geospatial information that is both useful to the attacker and not readily available from alternative sources should be subjected to the third filter, which considers the likely societal benefits and costs of restricting public access to this potentially sensitive information. For example, is public access required for local public safety needs?

Once decisionmakers proceed through the framework and determine that a particular piece of information may need to be restricted, they face the question of how to limit public access. This determination will depend on additional considerations because a variety of options as well as precedents exist for restricting public access to federal geospatial information sources. In addition, since our analysis showed that geospatial information is spread across a diverse range of federal and nonfederal sources, controlling any particular type of geospatial data could be challenging. If the objective were to enhance security, imposing information controls would be complicated by the likelihood in most cases that potential attackers could exploit diverse sources of geospatial and other types of relevant information.

Ultimately, these decisions, particularly those concerning the societal costs of restricting access, are neither easy nor exact. Evaluations of the benefits of geospatial information being publicly accessible are not readily available. Unfortunately, comprehensive or in-depth studies assessing the specific value of keeping such information publicly accessible have not yet been conducted and accepted.

Nonetheless, our framework provides a useful step in developing a consistent and uniform analytical process for federal agency decisionmakers to identify key considerations in making decisions on restricting public access to geospatial information.

Broader Implications

In addition to the specific findings, several broader implications emerged from our analysis. The following observations speak to broader aspects on the nature of geospatial information sources, the usefulness of geospatial information for potential attackers on U.S. homeland locations, and the role that the federal government could play in providing guidance to agencies about whether and how to restrict such information:

The ability of potential attackers to exploit publicly available geospatial information significantly varies with the type of information needed. With some important exceptions, the geospatial information needed for identifying and locating potential targets is widely accessible. In comparison, detailed and up-to-date information required for attack planning against a particular target is much less readily available from publicly available sources. A diverse range of geospatial data and information sources exist that could be exploited by attackers trying to meet their target identification information needs. Given the ready availability of alternative data sources, restricting public access to such geospatial information is unlikely to be a major impediment for attackers in gaining the needed information for identifying and locating their desired targets in the United States. The key exception to this general expectation is any type of geospatial information that reveals the location of vulnerabilities in the critical infrastructure that are not obvious or widely known, such as a particular choke point in a major power grid or telecommunications network. Compared with the ready availability of information that permits target identification and location, useful attack planning information for a particular critical infrastructure facility is much more difficult to find in publicly available sources. Given this condition of "information scarcity," any publicly available sources providing this type of detailed and timely information (e.g., internal facility equipment layout details, specifics on the security perimeter) should be more closely examined concerning their potential sensitivity for homeland security.

Our results do not rule out the possibility that federal publicly available geospatial information could be exploited by potential attackers, including the possibility that discrete pieces of such information could be aggregated by the attacker with the aim of achieving greater targeting value than is apparent when the information is viewed separately. However, these pieces of information should be identified in the context of how they might be specifically used by potential attackers. In addition, because widely available nonfederal sources often exist with similar geospatial information, alternative sources need to be assessed. Therefore, an analytical process is needed to evaluate individual geospatial datasets concerning their potential risks for protecting U.S. critical sites and whether restricting public access to certain parts of, or all of, the datasets would enhance homeland security.

Decisions about whether and how to restrict geospatial information would benefit from applying an analytic framework to help assess the sensitivity of a piece of geospatial information being publicly available and the security benefits and societal costs of restricting public access. The analytical approach presented in this study integrates three distinct filters—usefulness, uniqueness, and societal benefits and costs—as a first-step framework for decisionmakers to help evaluate whether a geospatial source is potentially sensitive and whether public access should be curtailed in some way. An explicit framework for analysis offers decisionmakers several benefits, including a way of making more structured and uniform decisions on whether and how to restrict public access to geospatial information and a better way of explaining the basis for such decisions to others.

Assessing the societal benefits and costs of restricting public access to geospatial information sources is not straightforward. Along with assessing the expected security benefits of restricting public access to certain types of information, our analytical framework seeks to weigh the societal costs of limiting public access. Most publicly available geospatial information addresses particular public and private needs for such information, including public safety, health, and economic development. For example, people working, recreating, or living near a critical site (e.g., chemical plants, gas pipelines) need geospatial information about a site to make decisions about accessing or avoiding the location when conducting their activities. However, gauging the costs of restricting public access is complicated by the limitations in existing methodologies for quantifying the specific benefits and costs of public access to geospatial information. Key decisions on restricting public access on geospatial information would be best made in a process that allows senior U.S. decisionmakers to make impartial judgments on the relative merits of these complex choices apart from the competing interests of stakeholders.

The federal government has a unique role in providing geospatial guidance to federal agencies, as well as insights on information sensitivity for nonfederal organizations. We conclude that civilian and military agencies have a growing need for well-founded and consistent guidelines for identifying geospatial data and information that could have homeland security implications. In addition, nonfederal organizations also need similar guidance in making decisions on information protection policies involving geospatial data and information.

General Recommendations

This report presents four general recommendations:

The federal government should play a proactive role in bringing greater coherence and consistency to assessing the homeland security implications of publicly available geospatial information. Federal agency staffs need practical guidance to assist them in framing choices about whether to place new restrictions on public access to parts of their geospatial information or to modify the restrictions imposed after the September 11 attacks.

An analytical process should be used by federal agencies and other organizations to assess the potential homeland security sensitivity of specific pieces of publicly available geospatial information and whether restricting access would enhance security. The analytical framework presented earlier is a useful first step that is immediately available for helping federal decisionmakers make sound and consistent assessments on whether and how to restrict public access to geospatial information for the purposes of enhancing U.S. homeland security. We also believe that this framework can be useful for any decisionmaker, not just federal ones, faced with the same type of determination.

For the longer term, the federal government should develop a more comprehensive model for addressing the security of geospatial information. A more formal and comprehensive model should be developed to provide a means of associating desired protection levels relative to the type of threats, relative protection profiles to defeat these threats, and a structured set of evaluation criteria. Facilities and installations could be, in turn, associated with those protection levels based on the particular needs of individual facilities and installations. Based on a process that integrates diverse expertise, a more comprehensive and formal model would provide public- and private-sector decisionmakers with a consistent level of protection for a wide variety of different types of facilities. It would also focus discussion away from how the data are to be protected to the more difficult question of what level of protection is appropriate for a given facility or installation.

In addition, the federal government should increase the awareness of the public and private sectors concerning the potential sensitivity of geospatial information. The federal government is uniquely positioned to generate and disseminate insights on the potential homeland security sensitivity of various types of geospatial data and information produced or distributed by a wide range of nonfederal organizations, including state and local governments, NGOs, and private-sector firms involved in geospatial activities or that operate critical infrastructure facilities.

Agency-Specific Recommendations

We expect that the Department of Homeland Security (DHS) and the Office of Management and Budget (OMB) will serve as lead policymaking agencies in formulating policy for U.S. federal agencies dealing with the homeland security implications of publicly available geospatial information. Similarly, as the lead homeland defense command operation, U.S. Northern Command (NORTHCOM) is likely to play a major role in providing guidance to a wide range of military decisionmakers concerned with force protection at U.S. installations.

However, as primary government agencies that produce and distribute geospatial data and information, the National Geospatial-Intelligence Agency (NGA, formerly the National Imagery and Mapping Agency) and the U.S. Geological Survey (USGS) of the Department of the Interior (DOI) could play a substantial role in applying their special expertise to help other organizations in identifying sensitive geospatial information. Both NGA and USGS possess unique capabilities and expertise relevant to helping the federal government develop guidelines for identifying sensitive geospatial information.

NGA should take advantage of its special expertise in geospatial intelligence to give other organizations a general sense of how various types of geospatial data and information could be exploited by potential adversaries for attacking U.S. critical infrastructure facilities and other key locations, including military installations. Specifically, NGA should leverage its expertise in such key areas as processing experience, military targeting, data integration, and knowledge of foreign geospatial information policies and practices.

Similarly, USGS can offer insights based on its relevant expertise in science-based applications and its strong sense of the breadth of domestic and international sources of publicly available geospatial information. USGS also has a good appreciation of the range of public and private stakeholders likely to be affected by any changes in public access to these types of data and information.

This report provides a framework for analysis that is relevant to decisionmakers who have responsibility for identifying and assessing geospatial information with homeland security implications. We conclude that there is a strong need for coherent and consistent guidelines to help federal agencies determine whether a specific piece of geospatial data and information is potentially sensitive and, if so, whether it should be considered for partial or complete restrictions concerning public access. Conversely, well-founded guidelines can also serve the public interest by giving decisionmakers a credible basis for modifying or dropping restrictions to geospatial sources in cases in which circumstances warrant such changes. In both instances, such guidelines should be shared with nonfederal public- and private-sector organizations that have similar responsibilities for managing public access to geospatial data and information that could have significant homeland security implications.

Acknowledgments

We would like to acknowledge the National Geospatial-Intelligence Agency for sponsoring this report, with particular thanks to its Office of the Americas. Our work benefited from the project team that NGA and its study partner on this report, the U.S. Geological Survey, brought together to review the research and analysis presented in this report. In addition to several experts at both agencies, we particularly express our thanks to Anita Cohen, Susan Kalweit, Monica Gaughan, and Laura Jennings at NGA, as well as Barbara Ryan and Michael Domaratz at USGS for their continuing involvement in guiding and encouraging this project.

Our study also gained important insights gained from discussions with geospatial experts at various levels of government, including the federal agencies (NGA, USGS, OMB, DHS, NASA, Office of Science and Technology Policy, DOI, EPA, DOT, and the U.S. Air Force). In addition, we benefited greatly from our interaction with the Federal Geographic Data Committee's Homeland Security Working Group, the various state and local government geospatial experts through discussions with the National States Geographic Information Council (NSGIC), and individual experts of several state and local governments ranging from several counties in Maryland to the City of New York.

The final report benefits greatly from reviews and comments by several knowledgeable reviewers, including Bruce Don, Murray Felsher, Kim Gavin, and John Young. In addition, numerous RAND colleagues made substantive, editorial, graphical, and administrative contributions to this report.

Any errors of fact or judgment that remain are solely those of the authors.

Abbreviations

9/11	September 11, 2001
BLM	Bureau of Land Management
BRS	Biennial Reporting System (EPA)
CBNR	chemical, biological, nuclear, and radiological weapons
CD-ROM	compact disk–read only memory
DEM	digital elevation model
DHS	Department of Homeland Security
DOC	Department of Commerce
DoD	Department of Defense
DOE	Department of Energy
DOI	Department of the Interior
DOQ	digital orthophoto quadrangle
DOT	Department of Transportation
EIA	Energy Information Administration
E-MAPS	Environmental Maps (HUD—Healthy Communities Environmental Mapping Initiative)
EPA	Environmental Protection Agency

FGDC	Federal Geographic Data Committee
GIS	geographic information system
GPS	Global Positioning System
GSD	ground sample distance
HUD	Department of Housing and Urban Development
INS	Inertial Navigation System
MMS	Minerals Management Service
MOU	Memorandum of understanding
NAPA	National Academy of Public Administration
NAPP	National Aerial Photography Program
NASA	National Aeronautics and Space Administration
NGA	National Geospatial-Intelligence Agency (formerly the National Imagery and Mapping Agency)
NGO	nongovernmental organization
NIST	National Institute of Standards and Technology
NOAA	National Oceanic and Atmospheric Administration
NORTHCOM	Northern Command
NRC	Nuclear Regulatory Commission
NSA	National Security Agency
NSDI	National Spatial Data Infrastructure
OMB	Office of Management and Budget
OSHA	Occupational Safety and Health Administration
PDD	Presidential Decision Directive
SAR	synthetic aperture radar

SCADA	Supervisory Control and Data Acquisition (information network)
TIGER	Topologically Integrated Geographic Encoding and Referencing system
TRI	Toxics Release Inventory (EPA)
UAV	unmanned aerial vehicle
USC	United States Code
USDA	Department of Agriculture
USGS	United States Geological Survey (DOI)

CHAPTER ONE

Introduction

Since the September 11, 2001 terrorist attacks on the U.S. homeland, federal government agencies have withdrawn some data and information that was publicly available before the attacks. These restrictions have included removing geospatial information from Web sites and federal depository libraries. Such steps reflect a substantially heightened concern that some types of publicly available geospatial information could make key U.S. facilities and locations more susceptible to attacks by terrorists or military adversaries. However, identifying which types of information might be exploited is challenging for two reasons. First, diverse types of geospatial data and information are publicly accessible from a wide range of sources. Second, fundamental uncertainty exists over what types of U.S. critical sites are likely to be targets for attack as well as how these potential targets could come under attack by terrorist groups or hostile foreign governments.

The federal government has major responsibilities for assessing the homeland security implications of publicly accessible geospatial data and information. One reason for this role is that the federal government has lead responsibility in, and special expertise for, dealing with terrorist attacks and foreign military threats. Second, federal agencies are major producers and distributors of geospatial data and information for a broad range of public purposes. Finally, information protection policies developed by the federal government for homeland security play an important role in establishing nationwide guidelines and practices through partnerships with state and local governments and with private-sector firms and nongovernmental organizations (NGOs).

This report assesses the U.S. homeland security implications of publicly available geospatial data and information—in particular, the implications for the federal government in its efforts to protect U.S. citizens and critical sites against potential terrorist threats. Geospatial data and information are used in identifying the geographical features of locations and facilities, as well as characterizing their important attributes, and are made publicly available by a wide range of government and private-sector organizations.

Our report frames the key issues in assessing how publicly available geospatial data and information from U.S. federal government sources might be used by terrorists and others in planning attacks on U.S. homeland locations. In particular, we assess whether the risks of effective attacks on critical U.S. sites increase if potential attackers exploit this geospatial information. We define critical sites in this report to include the full range of facilities and structures associated with the U.S. critical infrastructure sectors and key national assets as follows:

- *Critical infrastructure sectors* (i.e., agriculture, food, water, public health, emergency services, government, defense industrial base, information and telecommunications, energy, transportation, banking and finance, chemical industry and hazardous materials, and postal and shipping)[1]
- *Key national assets* (e.g., locations of cultural significance [national monuments, major sporting events, etc.], special event locations, military installations).

The report presents a framework for analysis that can assist decisionmakers in identifying potentially sensitive geospatial information

---

[1] In this report (The White House, 2003, pp. 6–7), the categories for critical infrastructure sectors match those outlined and being used by U.S. homeland security planners, while the key assets categories have been expanded somewhat to include military installations and special event locations involving any large population gatherings.

and in deciding on whether and how to restrict public access to such information.

Assessing the Homeland Security Implication of Geospatial Information

Following the September 11 attacks, federal government agencies took a new look at information protection policies, including those for geospatial information, to ensure that information being made publicly accessible by federal agencies did not help potential adversaries in planning attacks on U.S. critical sites—namely, various types of critical infrastructure facilities and other key locations. These steps have signaled an appreciation among top decisionmakers that the U.S. homeland is more vulnerable to direct attacks than was previously recognized. In this regard, a recent White House report on the homeland security strategy noted the particular challenges of protecting the nation's physical infrastructure:

> The September 11 attacks demonstrated our national-level physical vulnerability to the threat posed by a formidable enemy-focused, mass destruction terrorism. The events of that day also validated how determined, patient, and sophisticated—in both planning and execution—our terrorist enemies have become. The basic nature of our free society greatly enables terrorist operations and tactics, while, at the same time, hinders our ability to predict, prevent, or mitigate the effects of terrorist acts. Given these realities, it is imperative to develop a comprehensive national approach to physical protection.[2]

After September 11, individual federal organizations withdrew some of their geospatial information that had been previously available to the public via agency Web sites and printed documents. These initial decisions were made under conditions of time pressures and without much top-level guidance. However, even under the best circum-

---

[2] The White House (2003, p. vii).

stances, several factors complicate the decisionmaker's task of determining which information sources have significant homeland security implications and, if so, whether some type of restrictions on public access are necessary.

First, geospatial data and information take diverse and dynamic forms. For example, geospatial information can include a road map, an address in a telephone book, an aerial image, a topographical map, text description of a facility's location in a document, or a data layer from a geographic information system (GIS) database. Table 1.1 provides examples of the variety of geospatial data and information products that exist. Based on this, our definition of geospatial information for this study was broad. The diversity of media includes traditional geospatial databases (such as GIS data layers), Web pages, electronic storage mediums (e.g., CD-ROMs), and more traditional hard-copy documents and maps.

Equally important, most types of geospatial information are publicly available from many sources. A myriad possible data sources exist, including federal agencies, state and local governments, NGOs, private firms, and academic institutions. Various international sources also provide geospatial information about U.S. critical sites. At the same time, geospatial data are becoming integrated into daily civil society and commercial activities in more complex forms. For example, free, online mapping services, such as MapQuest, combine maps and overhead images, and cellular phones are now capable of receiving GPS (Global Positioning System) data, integrating with GIS datasets and displaying user-friendly maps. These examples also illustrate how the technologies are changing and how information is being developed and used in new ways.

In addition, in recent years, the advent of advanced information dissemination technologies, such as the personal computer and the World Wide Web, has greatly accelerated a trend toward "information abundance." Public institutions, private firms, NGOs, and even individuals have all contributed to the growing production and dissemination of geospatial data and information.

Table 1.1
Examples of Geospatial Data and Information Products

Types of Geospatial Product	Examples of Publicly Available Data and Information Products
Raw data	• Latitude and longitude coordinates • GPS coordinates
Maps and nautical charts	• U.S. Geological Survey (USGS) 1:24,000-scale topographic maps • National Oceanic and Atmospheric Administration (NOAA) nautical charts • Road maps
Overhead images	• Civilian and commercial satellite images (e.g., Landsat, SPOT, IKONOS) • Commercial aerial images
Datasets	• Housing data • Census datasets • Environmental Protection Agency (EPA) Toxics Release Inventory
Textual descriptions	• Web sites • Environmental Impact Statements • Historical descriptions • Telephone books

Along with the diversity of sources, geospatial information is highly dynamic, since new types arise and datasets are constantly being added to the already copious amount of existing geospatial data and information sources.

Thus, to formulate sound information protection policies, U.S. decisionmakers must take into account the vast diversity of the types and sources of geospatial information available to potential attackers.

Second, substantial uncertainty exists over what types of information potential attackers require. U.S. critical sites could be targeted by a broad range of terrorist groups and hostile foreign governments, both of which have access to very different information resources. The types of information required is also likely to vary by the intended target, whether it is a critical infrastructure site, a government facility, or another location where large population gatherings occur. In addition, the attacker's information requirements could diverge considerably depending on the planned attack mode (e.g., truck bomb, aircraft delivery, area weapon). Further, access to mission-critical information is often straightforward, as potentially useful attack information on many critical sites can be acquired through direct public access or observation. The interest of attackers in geospatial information is likely to be influenced by the degree of public access they can exploit in gaining needed information on critical U.S. sites. Appendix D categorizes critical U.S. sites by the degree of accessibility to critical infrastructure facilities and other key assets in terms of publicly accessible locations (e.g., train stations, bridges); limited access sites (e.g., energy generation plants, military installations), which are susceptible to direct observation from beyond their perimeters or through overflights; and restricted access sites that deny external observers almost any way of directly collecting useful information on their layout and operations. Thus, decisionmakers must consider a broad range of possibilities in assessing what types of geospatial information could have significant homeland security implications.

Third, decisions to restrict public access to geospatial information will involve both societal benefits and costs. The main benefit of restricting public access to geospatial information should be to improve U.S. homeland security against potential attacks. However, information that is publicly accessible often serves a broad range of public and private purposes. These purposes can range from performing public safety functions (e.g., maritime navigation) to supporting commercial services of various types. Decisionmakers must therefore consider both the expected homeland security benefits and the potential societal costs in weighing whether and how to restrict public access to geospatial information.

Public Access to Geospatial Information

Decisions to restrict publicly available geospatial information from federal agencies will be made against the backdrop of U.S. federal information policies, which have long been predisposed to making basic geospatial data and information on natural features, industrial installations, population centers, and other important features widely accessible.

In general, apart from sensitive information, such as national security information or personal information on individuals, U.S. federal data policy is committed to making data publicly accessible and to encouraging the widest possible distribution of information. The expectation is that citizens will benefit from the broad availability of such information for public safety and health, economic well-being, and the rights of citizens in a democracy to know what their federal government agencies are doing. In addition, efforts to improve the efficiency of citizen dealings with federal agencies are likely to involve a high degree of public access to federal government information. In the area of geospatial data and information, for example, the U.S. government is committed to developing the National Spatial Data Infrastructure (NSDI) based on a "standard core set of digital spatial information for the Nation that will serve as a foundation for users of geospatial information."[3] Further, a central feature of the NSDI is the establishment of a National Geospatial Clearinghouse, which uses the World Wide Web and a distributed network of clearinghouse server nodes in all U.S. states and U.S. regions, making various geospatial information available to governmental, nonprofit, and private-sector participants worldwide who wish to make their spatial information accessible on the Internet.

Other federal distribution mechanisms exist for making information publicly available. These include the Government Printing Office publication system, which includes more than 1,000 federal depository libraries dispersed throughout the United States and, increasingly, online information and databases publicly accessible through a wide variety of U.S. federal government agencies and offices.

Of course, U.S. federal agencies are not the only sources of geospatial data and information. Among the important producers and

---

[3] See OMB (2002).

distributors of unrestricted geospatial information are state and local government agencies, private-sector firms, universities, and NGOs. These nonfederal sources have a symbiotic relationship with their federal counterparts. Such organizations often make use of geospatial data and information produced by federal agencies and distribute it more widely and, at times, add value to such information to create new information products. Similarly, there is a trend toward federal agencies leveraging the growing geospatial capabilities found at other levels of government and in the private sector. For example, some state and local governments produce their own geospatial data and information that are sometimes more detailed and timely compared with those made publicly available by federal agencies.[4] Thus, any analysis on identifying potentially sensitive information for homeland security purposes needs to take into account that federal agencies are the leading—but not the only—sources of geospatial data and information that could be related to an extensive range of critical U.S. sites.

Research Objectives

Compelling reasons exist for assessing whether potential adversaries can take advantage of geospatial data and information for planning and executing effective attacks against critical sites in the U.S. homeland. Sound information protection policies for geospatial data and information can be an integral element of a broader, multitiered protection strategy for safeguarding the national critical infrastructure and other key assets from physical attacks. In response, the National Geospatial-Intelligence Agency (NGA, formerly the National Imagery and Mapping Agency) asked the RAND Corporation to undertake an independent assessment of how geospatial data and

---

[4] Similarly, an estimated 85 percent of the U.S. critical infrastructure and key assets are owned and operated by the private sector, making private industry an important partner in developing effective information protection policies and practices (The White House, 2003, p. 8).

information that is publicly available through federal government and other sources can affect the level of vulnerability of U.S. homeland facilities to physical attacks. Specifically, RAND's research approach focused on the following tasks:

- *Analyze publicly available geospatial information.* This task involved characterizing the basic types of geospatial data and information that are publicly available through U.S. federal agencies and identifying which sources are relevant to the U.S. critical infrastructure and other important locations. It also involved comparing these sources of information with what is available from other sources, such as state and local government agencies and private firms.
- *Assess information needs of potential attackers attacking U.S. sites.* This task involved assessing the vulnerability of the U.S. critical infrastructure and other potential targets to attacks by terrorists or foreign military forces. In addition, it involved identifying key information parameters that could affect the expected effectiveness of adversary attacks on U.S. homeland targets.
- *Evaluate potential benefits and costs of restricting access.* This task required analyzing the types of publicly available geospatial information with potential effects on the vulnerability of U.S. homeland targets. It also involved assessing the benefits and costs of restricting public access to certain geospatial datasets or information.
- *Develop a set of criteria for evaluating homeland security risks of publicly accessible geospatial information.* This task involved identifying the types of criteria that U.S. decisionmakers can use for evaluating the homeland security risks of having certain types of geospatial information that are publicly accessible.

The research undertaken on these tasks led to the development of an initial framework for analysis that helps U.S. decisionmakers identify publicly available geospatial information that could present risks for protecting homeland security.

Because of the potentially open-ended nature of each of these tasks, our main objective was to "frame the problem" by assessing the possible sensitivity of publicly available federal geospatial information for the vulnerability of U.S. homeland locations. Given NGA's tasking guidance and project time constraints, the study did not address the following issues, which fall outside the scope of this project's main focus:

- information without a direct or indirect geospatial characteristic (e.g., cyberinformation)
- classified information and nonpublic information (e.g., company proprietary information)
- data and information that is classified or withheld from the public under the Freedom of Information Act because of homeland security and national security purposes
- new and potentially sensitive information that might be created by integrating diverse data sources
- rationales for restricting public access to geospatial information for nonsecurity purposes.

Research Methodology

Our study approach focuses on identifying and assessing the key factors likely to determine the homeland security implications of geospatial data and information. We used a "demand" and "supply" approach to the problem by comparing publicly accessible geospatial data and information sources with the likely information needs of potential attackers of U.S. critical sites.

Demand-Side Methodology

On the demand side, this study identifies, in principle, the types of essential information that potential attackers, such as terrorist groups, would most likely require to have a high confidence in executing a major attack against U.S. homeland facilities or locations. We focused on answering two key questions:

- What kinds of information does an attacker need for target selection and identification and for attack planning purposes?
- How much will the attacker's essential information needs vary by changing the choice of target, type of attack mode, or desired attack objective?

We gained insights on the various types of information that attackers are likely to find most useful by analyzing a series of postulated attacks against various U.S. homeland targets, including (1) a critical infrastructure facility, (2) a military installation, and (3) a cultural location featuring a large public gathering.[5] Each attack analysis was based on rationales derived from plausible motivations, historic preferences for attack modalities by a number of real-world organizations, opportunities associated with some weapon systems that are becoming more widespread, and use of modern techniques and geotechnologies for targeting (e.g., remote sensing, geospatial information systems, GPS, range finders). We quantitatively evaluated each attack in terms of the likely damage against the target. The three analyses provided useful insights on the varied types of information that attackers could need, including both geospatial and nongeospatial, for attempting attacks on various U.S. critical sites.

Supply-Side Methodology
On the supply side of the equation, we analyzed the broad range of publicly available geospatial data and information sources to address the following key questions:

- What geospatial information about U.S. critical sites is publicly available from U.S. federal sources?
- How useful is this information, given attackers information needs?
- Is this information relatively unique or readily available from other nonfederal sources?

---

[5] Results of detailed targeting analyses were used to inform the broad findings presented in this report; however, these cases are not presented in this unclassified report.

- How significant (i.e., both useful and unique) is publicly available geospatial information from federal sources for addressing attackers' information needs?

After pursuing these areas, we combined the insights gained from the supply and demand analyses to assess the significance of federal geospatial information for addressing the attackers' information needs for target selection and identification or for planning an attack on U.S. critical sites. Our study approach involved an interactive process between the team members charged with the demand tasks and those with the supply tasks. This parallel approach of assessing demand aspects and supply aspects separately and then comparing results had certain benefits. These included generating independent assessments of the demand and supply problem before engaging in the necessary interactive process to evaluate the potential utility of publicly available geospatial information sources for addressing the information needs of possible attackers.

The research for this study was conducted from spring 2002 through spring 2003. A data collection phase occurred during spring and summer 2002, followed by an analysis phase through spring 2003. It is important to note that all information within this report was accurate at that time. However, given the dynamic nature of federal organizations and publicly available information, some of the specific examples cited may have changed over time.

Need for an Analytical Framework

The insights provided by both the demand and supply analyses were instrumental in developing a framework for analysis for decisionmakers responsible for identifying geospatial information with homeland security implications and deciding on whether and how to restrict public access to such information. An analytical framework provides an explicit and uniform process to assist the numerous U.S. decisionmakers responsible for making publicly available geospatial information that is relevant to U.S. critical sites, including critical infrastructure facilities and other key assets (e.g., national monuments, military installations). These decisionmakers must consider the homeland security implications of the geospatial information that their organizations make publicly available, which could be exploited by potential attackers.

An analytical framework is very relevant to the needs of civilian and military agencies responsible for developing information protection strategies for U.S. critical sites. For example, Department of Defense (DoD) installation managers need to be aware of which types of geospatial information concerning their installations are publicly accessible from other sources, as well as which types of potentially sensitive information, including geospatial information, that their organization should avoid making publicly accessible for force protection reasons.

Besides federal decisionmakers, this analytical framework is pertinent to a wide range of other geospatial information distributors, including organizations that produce and distribute geospatial information (e.g., state and local government agencies, private firms, NGOs, and academic institutions). Their decisionmakers also make determinations as to which types of information their organizations make publicly available. As partners in developing the nation's homeland security protection against physical attacks, these nonfederal organizations look to the federal government for advice and guidance on how to identify information that could be exploited by potential adversaries.

Using an explicit and uniform analytical process could offer several benefits, including:

- *Greater consistency* in how sensitive geospatial information is restricted by different federal organizations. At present, inconsistencies can arise from using uncoordinated approaches (both among and within agencies) for assessing the homeland security implications of publicly available geospatial information.
- *Coherently weighing all key factors,* which will reduce the chances that decisionmakers will overlook important—but less obvious—considerations.

- *Presenting an explicit rationale* for agency decisions, which should reduce misunderstandings and increase public confidence over why public access to certain types of geospatial information must be curtailed, at least in some ways, for homeland security reasons.
- *Encouraging a common information protection approach* through the use of an analytical process that presents standard criteria that federal and nonfederal decisionmakers should weigh in assessing the homeland security sensitivity of geospatial information that their organizations make publicly accessible.

Since the September 11 attacks, U.S. federal decisionmakers and others clearly have had a pressing need for a framework for analysis that can help them identify and assess the homeland security implications of publicly accessible geospatial information. Thus, this study draws on the insights gained from the demand and supply analysis of attackers' information needs and the nature of publicly accessible geospatial information to develop an analytical framework that identifies key criteria for assessing the homeland security implications of publicly accessible geospatial information. Although a more formal, comprehensive model is desirable over the longer term, the framework serves as an initial step that is immediately available for developing a more uniform and structured approach to assessing the homeland security implications of publicly accessible geospatial information generated by federal agencies and other sources.

How the Report Is Organized

The next four chapters of this report present our analysis and findings on the homeland security implications of publicly available geospatial data and information. Chapter Two analyzes the demand side of the problem by considering the key information needs of terrorist groups and hostile governments seeking to attack critical sites in the U.S. homeland. Chapter Three provides an in-depth analysis of the supply side of the equation by first characterizing which types of geospatial data and information are available from U.S. federal government sources and then analyzing their potential significance for satisfying the information needs of attackers. Chapter Four offers a framework for identifying potentially sensitive geospatial data and information using a series of analytical filters. The report's conclusions and recommendations are presented in Chapter Five. Additional supporting material is located in the appendices.

CHAPTER TWO

What Are the Attackers' Key Information Needs?

Assessing the potential benefits of strategies for safeguarding geospatial information requires an understanding of how a potential enemy could use the protected data. However, it is not enough merely to assess whether these data could be used for malevolent purposes, since this determination neglects whether there are alternative sources to access comparable information and substantially fulfill the attacker's needs as well as the possible benefits of such information.[1] To assess an attacker's information requirements, it is necessary to understand an attacker's objectives, possible targets, modes of attack, and how effective such an attack might be. Only with this information is it possible to appraise properly the likely benefits of protecting against an adversary's use of geospatial information.

This chapter highlights our general approach to the problem of identifying attackers' information needs and presents our top-level findings on the utility of protecting different classes of information. The first section of the discussion examines the problem of defining the threat space, as well as the critical decision as to how effective the defense needs to be against the threat. The second section looks at the basic information needs of the attacker for both target selection and

---

[1] The concern over the possible misuse of information or technology is not a new one. As Bishop John Wilkins wrote in his discussion of cryptography *Mercury, or The Secret and Swift Messenger* (1641): "If all those useful Inventions that are liable to abuse, should therefore be concealed, there is not any Art or Science which might be lawfully profess." This issue will be particularly relevant as consideration is advanced toward the issues of data aggregation and the tools through which the data are manipulated.

attack planning. The third section discusses in a general way a case study of how attackers' selection of attack modalities and their information needs interact. The last section draws out some of the challenges confronting any defender using an information protection strategy, in attempting to thwart an attacker who can simply shift objectives and means of attack.

Methodology

As discussed earlier, our study examines both the demand and supply sides of geospatial information. This chapter focuses on the demand side of the equation and places the demand for geospatial information within the broader context of the information needs of the attacker. The approach to targeting, as well as the variety of weapons considered for the attack, was designed to capture the spectrum of possible approaches an attacker might use and alternate ways in which the targets might be attacked.

To gain insights to the key information needs of potential attackers against the U.S. homeland, we undertook an analysis involving a series of postulated attacks against a spectrum of critical infrastructure, military targets, and cultural and social targets of possible interest. The rationales for the attack were derived from plausible attacker motivations, historic preferences for attack modalities by a number of real-world organizations, opportunities associated with some weapon systems that are proliferating more widely, and use of modern techniques and tools for targeting (e.g., remote sensing, geospatial information systems, GPS, range finders). These attacks were quantitatively evaluated in terms of the likely damage they would have on the target. Our evaluation used conventional U.S. weapon effects assessment techniques, such as using the Joint Munitions Effectiveness Manual for conventional military ordnance, to assess the effectiveness of the attack. The thresholds for success or failure of the attack were derived from objectives laid out for the attacker. To capture the flavor of possible enemy targeting approaches, we avoided mirror imaging the U.S. approach to targeting (particularly in regard to the strong focus on avoiding collateral damage and achieving an economy of force).[2] This allowed for the research team to investigate possible attacks inconsistent with U.S. norms but well within the capabilities and practices of other parties.

Results from this phase of the analysis were used to help evaluate the potential usefulness of geospatial information sources uncovered in the supply-side portion of the analysis (see Chapter Three). While our targeting analysis was limited to a small number of end-to-end case studies that tracked attacks from the formulation stage through the attack and assessed their direct impact in the target, we were able to draw a fairly clear picture of how possible attackers might utilize geospatial information sources in the planning and execution of attacks. The results of this broad picture of how potential enemy planners could make use of geospatial data allow for a first-order assessment of how withholding such data might affect or alter attacker plans.

Defining the Threat Space

A key element in developing an information protection strategy is having a clear understanding of the attacker's information demands. Even a cursory examination immediately reveals that no single threat profile exists against which to operate. Potential attackers run the gamut from small groups with little intelligence support and access to rudimentary weaponry, to groups with some indigenous capability for intelligence gathering and access to military weaponry, to hostile governments with access to the full spectrum of weapons and intelligence-gathering methods. There are also possible pairings between terrorist groups and nation-states that could enable even poorly

---

[2] A good discussion of basic targeting principles can be found in U.S. Department of the Air Force (1998). The report lays out fundamentals of targeting and provides a good example of rational (goal-oriented) targeting practices.

equipped and organized groups to receive some of the benefits of access to a national intelligence organization. The implications of all these pairings are quite important in thinking about information protection strategies. If one's opponent is able to gather information independently, easily, with high confidence, and with minimal risk of exposure, then withholding information is not likely to present substantial obstacles for the attacker.

Each of the different types of attackers offers a different sort of challenge to the defender. At the top end of the spectrum, hostile governments have the benefits of access to support from state intelligence services capable of gathering information from a potentially broad set of open and closed sources. Farther down the threat level are organized terrorist organizations that can use intelligence gathered by nation-state patrons, can gather some open source information, and can also conduct selective human intelligence and social engineering collection activities. At the bottom end of the spectrum are individuals who generally would be able to use open-source information when available but would necessarily have a much more focused type of collection activity because of their limited resources.

Given the spectrum of information-gathering resources available to prospective attackers, strategies designed to protect targets by hiding or obscuring information are likely to have quite different effects, depending on the attacker. A strategy that might be able to hide information from an individual with limited time and resources might prove completely ineffective against an adversary with access to even a modest sum of money to purchase commercial aerial or space imagery, high-quality industry data, or with the appropriate equipment and necessary patience to obtain similar information. Similarly, efforts designed to thwart the mid-level attack may not be particularly effective against more sophisticated and well-equipped adversaries capable of gathering information using extensive open-source, overt, and clandestine collection approaches.

The Attacker:
Motivations, Strategies, and Modalities of Attack

In considering what the United States should do in terms of protecting its geospatial information from use in an attack, it is necessary to understand something of the possible nature of such an attack. Three major vectors can characterize the attacker effectively: (1) motivations, (2) strategies to achieve desired end states, and (3) means of attack to achieve those ends. While an explicit assessment of the motivations of attackers is outside the scope of this study, it is useful to consider briefly why the attacker might be conducting an attack because it will help define some possible contexts for employing weapons. Furthermore, such analysis offers insights on the abilities of adversaries to shift their strategy and means of attack as needed to accommodate limitations in information-gathering capabilities.

The various possible motivations are important because they show that, from the outset, possible attackers may have one or more of a broad range of possible objectives. Thus, the defender must be prepared to deal with a wide range of possible strategies.[3]

Some possible attacker objectives might be

- coercion directed at the United States
- coercion directed at a third party
- economic damage
- military damage
- boosting the morale of the attacking party
- chaos.

It is difficult to generalize about the specific objectives of attackers. There are many different possible attackers and many different possible objectives as well as associated means for achieving these

---

[3] A defense can only be deemed as successful if it meets the defender's objectives, not simply interfering with the ability of the attacker reaching its objective. However, for our purpose of understanding what an attacker might do, the above exercise of thinking about the diversity of attacker objectives is still useful in considering the possible impact of an information protection strategy.

objectives. Certain from the standpoint of the defense is that there is a hefty list of possible motivations. Also, there are likely to be quite different thresholds for success or failure among the actors. For some, a bomb detonating near a target may be sufficient, while for others, a specific kind of damage (e.g., mass casualties) might be required. Indeed, the latter may be especially true for primarily political and psychological objectives in which the battle is largely one of perceptions.

The Attacker's Tool Box: Types of Weapons Considered

Attackers possess a wide range of possible modes of attack, all of which relate to the information available to the attacker. For the purposes of this study, we identified four main categories of attack that connect to the amount of detailed information needed on the target (see Table 2.1).

The first option—direct attack—reflects the most precise type of attack, with the weapon having to be placed extremely close to the desired aimpoint. The damage caused could be broad in effect, but in general the attack achieves its effect by applying the damaging energies against a precise point.

The second option reflects a precision attack using higher-order damage mechanisms. This category captures the use of explosives that allow some standoff from the ideal aimpoint while still achieving the desired damage expectancy. Here the key is using humans in the control loop of the weapon to allow for dynamic aimpoint refinement and for selecting the aimpoint while the weapon is inbound to the target. In some cases, this man-in-the-loop tactic might consist of an individual steering a vehicle loaded with explosives into the designated target.

The third case captures the use of autonomous weapons. Here the weapon requires precise targeting information, which puts a greater burden on the preflight mission planning process. These weapons could include UAVs, cruise missiles, or ballistic missiles with

Table 2.1
Modes of Attack

Direct attack	• Demolition charges • Anti-materiel rifles • Sabotage of sensitive components
Man-in-the-loop precision attack	• Suicide vehicular attack (air, land, sea) • Suicide bomber • Unmanned aerial vehicle (UAV) with data link for human operator
Autonomous precision attack	• Aircraft using GPS/Inertial Navigation System (INS) • UAV using GPS/INS • Cruise missiles using GPS/INS • Ballistic missiles using GPS/INS
Area attack	• Chemical, radiological, biological agents from platforms • Ad hoc chemical and radiological release • Nuclear weapon

guidance systems not requiring inputs after launch. In all these cases, the weapon is expected to guide itself to a designated aimpoint loaded into the guidance systems. The most likely high-quality guidance system to be used by adversaries would be an inertial navigation unit combined with a GPS system. This allows the significant reduction of in-flight navigation errors and greatly increases the chance of the target being struck successfully.

Finally, the last category concerns weapons with very large areas of impact, such as chemical, biological, radiological, nuclear, or high-yield explosive (CBRNE) threats. In terms of targeting information, this category requires very minimal information for effective employment. There can be a strong dependency on detailed geospatial information if some of the weapons are employed in a precision-attack role for, say, targeting a critical building with a small amount of material. But in general, the last category stresses information needs in other specialized areas, such as that for timely local weather information, in place of more traditional geospatial information.

Of the four categories, the first three are of greatest interest in considering an information protection strategy. The last category—

area attacks—includes weapons of such broad impact that it is less useful to include in our analysis. Even if the area attack involves employing such weapons precisely, the required information needs would already be captured in the other three categories, which focus on direct accurate placement of the munitions.

Given these primary attack categories, we next turn to the inter-connections among the possible objectives, attack modalities, and information requirements.

A General Model of Attacker Information Needs

As seen in Table 2.2, an attacker's information needs can be generally distinguished by two distinct domains: those concerned with infor-mation useful to selecting a target type and even a specific type loca-tion, and those concerned with the details of planning the attack against the selected targets. As we discuss later, this distinction is use-ful because of the contrasting situation of "information abundance"

Table 2.2
Illustrative Attacker Information Needs

Target-selection information	• Which target? • Where is it in general? • What effect can the attacker achieve with a given class of attack and weapon?
Targeting and attack information	• Is the target located where the attacker expects it to be such that the attack can be delivered effectively? • What is the target made of, and how thick are the walls? • What does the facility look like today, so the attacker can recognize it? • Where are the guards, and how are they armed? • Is there a quick reaction force? • Is there a ditch that the attacker can use for cover?

for target selection and "information scarcity" for the very specific information that attackers need to have high confidence in to accomplish their mission. This table highlights the distinctive types of information that attackers require by presenting illustrative questions that need to be addressed in undertaking effective attacks.

By target selection, we mean the process by which attackers identify a target that is consistent with their broad objectives and strategy. The target class (e.g., chemical plant, bridge, building) is largely dictated by the basic selection of an objective and strategy, while the particular target may be dictated by the ability of the attacker to identify the particular element, such as a particular set of storage tanks that are vulnerable to attack. For example, assuming that the attackers are interested in disrupting U.S. economic activity to demonstrate the impotence of U.S. homeland security measures, they might identify some critical infrastructure elements as the key leverage point based on a combination of analysis and prior beliefs on how the American system functions. With a target class selected, the next step would be selecting a node for attack. Here, information on exact location of critical links, and the locations of particularly susceptible target elements, is important.

Thus, our assessment is that there is a tremendous amount of information generally available that is useful for target selection. Many of the targets of possible interest are readily identifiable by simple observation either through direct access or from remote locations. However, compared with the information required for general target identification, the information necessary for attack planning is substantially more detailed and not as widely disseminated as that for selecting targets. Here, the information requirements are closely linked to the modes of attack and the desired impact of the attack. If the attack is to be executed by a ground force, a great deal of detailed information might be required for the attacking party to gain access to the facility. Specifics on ground cover, possible defensive strong points, entryways, and other features predominate. If, however, the attacker plans an air attack using a suicide or remote controlled vehicle, the primary information requirements would be aerial orientation, obstruction data, and key aimpoints. In most cases, the attacker would be interested in collecting information with a high degree of currency to increase confidence in undertaking an effective attack.

For targets that allow public access (as do the vast majority of possible targets in the United States), there is a tremendous amount of information that is available or that could be gathered with little difficulty by an attacker. These targets are located in "publicly accessible locations" that allow potential attackers to observe both internal and external features. Indeed, most of the attacker's reconnaissance activities are likely to be very low risk and would provide information at least as useful as that available in any of the publicly accessible databases. The direct observation data would probably be superior in most cases because it would have greater currency and could be tailored to the attacker's needs.

Against more heavily protected installations that do not allow unfettered access, however, attackers would need to gather information from beyond the perimeter area. They might take advantage of remote sensing systems that include observation from terrain or nearby man-made features, the air, and even space. Examples of such limited-access sites include many DoD and industrial facilities. Even here, the combination of publicly available data and the use of even modest remote observation capabilities can be quite useful to the attacker. For instance, while interior details of an installation may be shielded, its external features can generally be well characterized. With the external information, and at least basic knowledge of the installation function and type, it is possible to construct a reasonable, if limited, model of internal installation layouts.

As with the more accessible installations, most reconnaissance efforts are likely to fall into the low-risk category. Some types of activities, which might require current and detailed ground-level reconnaissance, might be interfered with by the defender, but then the attacker is under no obligation to limit its attack modalities to those that require such information.

Gathering information on denied areas (i.e., protected and concealed installations) is quite a different proposition for the attacker and would be more demanding and risky. The United States possesses only a relatively small number of locations, such as high-security government installations, that could be considered denied areas. Here, external observation of the installation may provide little help in understanding the target, either because the installation is intentionally sheltered to prevent observation, or, as in the case of underground facilities, it is hardened in a manner that prevents external observation. Consequently, even knowledge of the installation's location may not offer much information that is useful in formulating a plan for attack. Clearly, other information sources beyond direct observation become very important, or the attacker has to resort to attack modes that are compatible with the limited information on the target.

Accessibility and Critical Sites

In principle, critical U.S. sites that are highly accessible are more vulnerable to a range of attack modes. In addition, greater accessibility presents attackers with more choices in obtaining needed information. For example, attackers are likely to desire firsthand information for ensuring the reliability and timeliness of their targeting data in undertaking their planned attacks.

The usefulness of publicly available geospatial information for potential attackers is probably driven by whether the attackers have other means for obtaining essential attack information on a particular site. These alternative means could include direct access or direct observation (e.g., reconnaissance using drive-by or flyover means). In cases in which such access or observation is readily available and can provide the necessary information, the usefulness of secondary source information, including publicly available geospatial information, is diminished. However, in other instances in which direct access and observation are impossible or involve an unacceptable risk of being detected, the publicly available geospatial information would likely have much greater appeal to attackers. Similarly, other types of secondary source information that provide insights into the potential system-level vulnerabilities within the critical infrastructure that are not readily apparent to outside observers could be valuable to potential attackers regardless of whether they can exploit public access to the corresponding critical sites.

Critical sites can be differentiated by the degree of public accessibility that is possible. Figure 2.1 illustrates one way of characterizing these differences by presenting three types of public access at critical sites that potential attackers could exploit for acquiring needed information. They are the following:

- *Publicly accessible locations,* or facilities and locations where public access is routinely expected. These include most transportation nodes and other key assets that depend on extensive public access (e.g., stadiums, monuments, commercial business centers). Substantial access creates opportunities for potential attackers, such as terrorists, to collect "eyes-on" information (or even photographs) without much risk of being readily recognized as potential threats.

Figure 2.1
Critical Sites by Degree of Public Accessibility

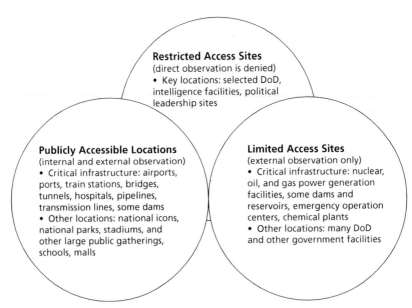

Restricted Access Sites
(direct observation is denied)
• Key locations: selected DoD, intelligence facilities, political leadership sites

Publicly Accessible Locations
(internal and external observation)
• Critical infrastructure: airports, ports, train stations, bridges, tunnels, hospitals, pipelines, transmission lines, some dams
• Other locations: national icons, national parks, stadiums, and other large public gatherings, schools, malls

Limited Access Sites
(external observation only)
• Critical infrastructure: nuclear, oil, and gas power generation facilities, some dams and reservoirs, emergency operation centers, chemical plants
• Other locations: many DoD and other government facilities

RAND *MG142-2.1*

- *Limited access sites*, most of which are industrial plants and government facilities, including most military installations in the continental United States, where public access is normally limited. Attempts to gain unauthorized access to these facilities involve the risk of being detected and caught. However, external observation of many sites is possible for potential attackers through ground-level (e.g., drive-by) reconnaissance or by use of aerial observation. Examples of limited access sites include nuclear, oil, and gas power generation facilities; some dams and reservoirs; emergency operations centers; and many DoD facilities.
- *Restricted access sites*, or those selected U.S. government facilities where both direct access and direct observation is denied through a combination of tightly controlled access policies, security perimeters with substantial setback from public roads, and restricted flight areas. Examples of these sites include some government facilities as well as political leadership locations where access is severely restricted, such as Camp David.

By far, most critical U.S. sites consist of locations where direct access or limited access is feasible. As a result, potential attackers are likely to have, in principle, opportunities for external observation of most critical sites and, in some cases, the opportunity for making internal observations (e.g., inside a rail station). Moreover, attackers are likely to exploit other information sources (publicly available or from, for example, insiders at a critical site) to build upon the type of information that can be derived from direct access and/or observation.

How the Attacker Acquires the Necessary Information

As we have seen, attackers have the ability to gather a substantial amount of information on targets for both target selection and attack planning. We can classify the information attackers might gather into two primary categories: "in-class" types of geospatial information (i.e., direct analogs, such as substituting aerial imagery for space-based imagery, of what might be found in conventional geospatial data sources), and "out-of-class" data sources, such as direct observation or "eyes on target" and social engineering. Of the two categories, we have found that the out-of-class sources, some of which have a geospatial component, represent some of the most profuse sources of information for a potential attacker. In-class sources for publicly available geospatial information, while useful in getting a broad view of a target system, tend to lack the specificity and currency useful in the final target selection and attack planning portion of the operations.

Drawing on the distinction between in-class and out-of-class information types, Table 2.3 lists illustrative information sources potentially available to attackers. Publications intended for broad consumption, particularly technical publications and trade journals,

Table 2.3
Illustrative Sources of Information

Information Type	Examples
Publications	• Technical publications • Company publications, annual reports • Trade journals and economic periodicals • Governmental publications • Equipment manuals
Human intelligence, social engineering	• Current employees • Former employees • Service and vendor personnel with access to target location
Direct observation	• Eyes-on reconnaissance or surveillance • Aided observation (e.g., telescope devices)
Photography and overhead imagery	• Still cameras or video cameras • Aerial photography or imaging • Commercial satellite imaging
Public databases	• Census data • Local government property records • Federal overhead imagery databases

provide a rich source of in-class or geospatial information that is useful to the general population as well as experts. Much of the information is applicable to understanding a target class in a fairly general sense and providing a potential attacker with an understanding of how an installation of a given class is put together and operates. This basic knowledge allows attackers to fill in gaps of knowledge on a particular installation with reasonable estimates. Trade journals, company publications, and equipment manuals can, with some effort and expertise, be combined to provide a comprehensive view of many targets. However, even with such diverse information sources, it is difficult to count on getting detailed knowledge of any particular target.

Controlling this basic information is problematic. To construct and operate most kinds of critical infrastructure, the basic knowledge of how the installations function, as well as general operational details, needs to be widely available. Furthermore, the basic information on most target types has been irretrievably disseminated to the world at large and is available in myriad forms. Even some of the most recently published information, which is largely located on Web sites, might have been copied and stored in many locations both inside and outside of U.S. control. Thus, any attempts to hide or withdraw the information for security protection purposes could prove to be futile at best. Furthermore, such ineffectual activities bring other disadvantages, including disrupting the functioning of the infrastructure, complicating critical infrastructure protection planning, and possibly leading to a false sense of security at worst.

Moving beyond intentionally published documents, we briefly discuss the application of social engineering and human intelligence in gathering information. This discussion is not about the use of covert insider information, but rather the process of gathering information through the observation of individuals and through elicitation. The kinds of information gathered here would essentially be private information unintentionally released by otherwise authorized individuals. This information could provide some very important insights on facility processes, procedures, and other activities that might not be widely publicized. Controlling such releases of information has been shown to be fairly difficult for most organizations because so much of the information is essentially benign and it requires employees to act in fairly atypical ways for the workplace. Also, there are likely to be adverse effects from restricting the information. As in the case of published information, effective controls would undoubtedly interfere with many legitimate activities and have a negative impact on the efficiency of facility operations.

Another powerful and difficult-to-control source of information comes from direct observation ("eyeballs"), aided observation, or remote observation of the possible target. As mentioned earlier, most targets are quite accessible, and the majority of those that cannot be directly approached can be observed from other locations using telescopic devices.[4] Indeed, many of the general features of potential target facilities are readily observed from the current generation of commercial satellite systems less than 1-meter GSD,[5] while details are readily discerned at less than 0.3-meter GSD in many aerial images. Both aerial and space-based imagery also allow for precise geolocation when used in conjunction with presurveyed ground control points and/or GPS onboard a vehicle used for observation.

Finally, publicly accessible databases also serve as possible information sources for attackers. As we discuss in detail in Chapter Three, much of the data are of a fairly general nature, from the attacker's perspective. The databases in question provide a convenient, if not unique, way of surveying potential target sets for target selection. However, serious gaps in existing public databases would still necessitate a broader information-gathering activity in planning an operation. In terms of attack planning, the gap is even greater. Uncertain data quality, limitations of the data, and possibly aged data

------

[4] If telescopic devices are combined with GPS and range-finding systems, they can create a very powerful real-time or near-real-time system suitable for both civil and military applications.

[5] Ground sample distance (GSD) relates to the pixel size and spatial resolution of imagery data.

would all require a prudent attack planner to gather a large quantity of supplemental information.[6]

Table 2.4 summarizes our key observations on attacker interaction with possible information sources. First, we must acknowledge that there is a great deal of information that will be available to the attacker. Second, because of the current information abundance, attacker knowledge of many fundamental facts cannot reliably be denied. Third, there may be some information that will not be widely known and, hence, can be protected in order to offer some defense of the target. This information protection probably will not be broad

Table 2.4
Key Observations: Attacker Interaction with Information Sources

Most information is already available via open sources, readily collectable sources, or low-risk clandestine operations	• Multitude of sources suggest that, at best, most data protections would have a minimal negative impact on attackers • Gaps in knowledge are likely to be bridged with expert knowledge
There is also a large set of information that cannot reasonably be protected	• Vulnerability assessment based on casual appraisal of data • Profound network vulnerabilities that are intrinsic in the basic architecture • Exploitable security vulnerabilities that can be found through probing
There exists a small subset of information that can reasonably be protected	• Vulnerability assessments based on deep knowledge of infrastructure • Network vulnerabilities that are transitory (e.g., "the backup system is down today") • Exploitable security deficiencies that are addressable by a defender over a short period

---

[6] A typical geospatial example would be the reported location of an installation. If latitude and longitude are reported, the question is frequently what point in the facility or installation is being reported. That is, most of the data sources do not report locations of subelements of the facility or installation but rather a single point. Is that point the facility or installation centroid, front gate, northwest corner, or some other point? Can the attacker assume with any real confidence that the location is correct? It seems likely a prudent planner would at least spot-check the data and in the process gather a great deal of other information.

but might still be useful. The next section of the chapter addresses the issues of why information protection strategies are likely to have only limited effects in diminishing attackers' abilities to strike effectively in support of their overall objectives.

Harmonizing Objectives, Attack Modalities, and Information Requirements

Motivations are intimately linked to the strategies and modes of attacks. Further, the range of possible attacker motivations, strategies, and modes has a significant impact on the usefulness to be gained from an information protection strategy. Attacks can be less discriminating in nature, by virtue of either the strategy or modality. Weapons like C-4 explosives can be used either very discriminately or indiscriminately, while something like a radiological device has much higher intrinsic collateral damage potential. If information is denied in the form of precision-targeting coordinates, the attacker can turn to a man-in-the-loop strategy to guide a weapon into a critical aim-point. Such an aimpoint could be identified based on first-principles analysis even when using lower-quality targeting data.

Take the example of a critical infrastructure target being attacked by a simple unitary weapon. We examined a sample attack to determine how decreasing the quality of geospatial information might affect an attack directed at a critical node. In this particular case, as shown in Figure 2.2, we parametrically varied the target location error (i.e., that associated with assigning the location of the target in latitude, longitude, and altitude) across a wide range of possible values. The error was varied from the precise levels that can be obtained using GPS (positioned at the site or used with a laser range finder), through remote sensing images ranging from what is typically seen in high-resolution aerial applications, through standard digital orthophoto quadrangles (DOQs)[7] available for mapping, all the way

---

[7] A digital orthophoto is a computer-generated image of an aerial photograph or satellite image in which displacements caused by camera orientation and terrain have been removed.

through Landsat[8] satellite images for very large targets. We then used standard weaponeering tools to assess the likelihood of particular damage criteria to be achieved by the attack. Figure 2.2 illustrates the results of the attack against a representative critical infrastructure target. In this case, and with many other critical infrastructure targets, we found that with prudent selection of aimpoints to focus on the larger elements of the target complex, the target location errors would not be large enough to protect a targeted site to significantly diminish the attacker's ability to achieve the desired level of damage. This example shows that, even when location error is allowed to increase to

Figure 2.2
Targeting Demands Can Be Satisfied with Even Medium-Resolution Geospatial Data Products

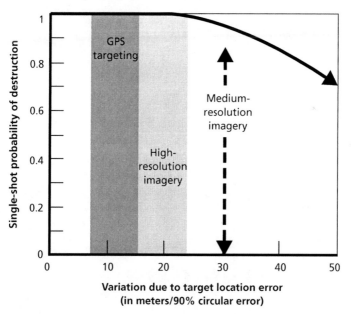

RAND *MG142-2.2*

---

[8] Landsat is a U.S. civil remote sensing satellite that provides images at moderate resolution (i.e., 15–30 meters).

the level typically associated with medium-resolution imagery controlled to a digital elevation model, the single-shot probability of kill exceeds 95 percent. Given that most attackers are likely to enjoy substantially better target location errors by using either direct observation aided with tools like GPS or geocoded imagery, it appears that attempts introducing errors are not likely to be very successful.

A critical point to keep in mind when considering the attacker-defender relationship is that attackers have many degrees of freedom, while defenders are greatly constrained. In this situation, the attackers have the potential advantage of flexible objectives, as well as substantial flexibility in terms of when and how targets are attacked. Thus, they will often have the "last move." This advantage is particularly important in considering the possibility that attackers might "satisfice"—that is, seek to obtain an outcome that is "good enough" —rather than optimize their attack. Satisficing attackers are likely to have available many possible attacks that meet their threshold of performance (picking from a number of options that meet a performance threshold), whereas optimizing attackers (picking the best based on a set of constraints) are likely to have a smaller number of possible attacks that meet their objective.

Because of this flexibility on the part of the attacker (i.e., the ability to choose why, where, how, and how good the attack needs to be), counterstrategies based on thwarting enemy objectives become intrinsically problematic.[9] Against such adversaries, information protection strategies—at least in terms of limiting the opponent's ability to strike at targets it thinks are most important—probably will have minimal impact.

Thus, our analysis offers several insights, including that the attacker often has the following characteristics:

------

[9] Take the example of an attack motivated by U.S. troop presence somewhere in the world. A possible attack against U.S. interests might be motivated by U.S. troop presence in a particular country, but attacks against the forces themselves would be too difficult. A U.S. critical infrastructure target might come into play as a morale-building exercise. The act of attacking, not the outcome, might be the important element. An attack might be quite successful for the attacker even if the tangible damage to the United States were minimal.

- wide variety of possible strategic objectives
- large number of modalities for attack
- large array of potential targets from which to choose
- an ability to undertake even "ineffectual" attacks that might be successful given some objectives
- little in the way of forcing functions
- working at his or her timescale (not the defender's timetable)
- operating below the noise floor until the attack occurs.

The primary point is that not only do the attackers enjoy the traditional advantage of maintaining the initiative, but they can also redefine the thresholds of success so broadly that any effort to prevent attacks against the expansive critical infrastructure target set will prove very difficult.

Lessons from Analysis of Attackers' Information Demands

While the above discussion on the problem of shifting objectives, attack modes, and thresholds of performance broadly addresses the question of whether geospatial information could be used by an attacker, it is central to the larger issue of *whether removing that information will substantially alter the frequency and effectiveness of attacks against the critical infrastructure targets.*

Based on our assessment presented in this chapter, we conclude that changing the availability of geospatial information would likely have only a minimal impact on the attacker's ability to strike, although it might have a slightly greater impact on effectiveness and/or propensity of striking a particular target. We have highlighted both attacker flexibility and broad definitions of attack "success" throughout this discussion. In all likelihood, if certain information were restricted, attacks would simply shift toward other, softer targets or would encourage the attacker to employ brute-force modes of attack that allow for adequate damage against the intended target using lower-quality information.

The end result is that there are large arrays of attacks that cannot be practically addressed through an information protection strategy. Therefore, is there no point of engaging in any kind of information protection strategy? *The answer to this question is no, because there are some kinds of information that should be protected, but very little of it is publicly available geospatial information per se.* However, much of that sensitive information may in the future be linked together inside geospatial information systems' databases as detailed attribute data. This sensitive attribute data contain the very small subset of data about details of the facility or installation useful for attack planning that, more than simply adding uncertainty to the attacker's plans, gives the defense an advantage in terms of countering and responding to the attack. As such, shielding this class of data would probably be central to an effective information protection strategy.

The defender inevitably has the weaker hand as long as the enemy can pick the time, place, and manner of the attack. However, the defense does have the option of engaging in preferential defense strategies that attempt to protect a subset of possible targets. Such strategies make sense if the defender is preserving a subset of capabilities that are not apparent to the attacker or will somehow ensure a critical capability is retained. Consider the case of protecting a telecommunications network. A strategy of combining information protection strategies, along with building redundancy into the system to absorb an attack and an active defense strategy, might allow for a high-confidence defense against many types of attacks. While either active defenses or redundancy alone might make a significant improvement of capability, information protection strategies tend to bolster the primary defensive approach rather than being an end in their own right. This means that any information protection strategy must be viewed as an element of a larger comprehensive protection strategy in which the protection will be properly traded off against other approaches to prevent, defeat, or recover from an attack.

Attackers Have Substantial Flexibility in Fulfilling Their Information Needs

On balance, our analysis has revealed a number of key points that offer some insights into how varying the amount and quality of geospatial information available to possible attackers might influence their operations against U.S. critical infrastructure and key assets as targets. The following insights highlight the basic flexibility advantage that attackers hold:

- Attackers have a great deal of flexibility in terms of why, where, and how they attack U.S. critical infrastructure and other key targets.
- Attackers can compensate for decreasing quality and amounts of information by shifting not only their modalities of attack (e.g., higher-yield weapons, man-in-the-loop weapons) but also their target classes and performance thresholds to adjust to the information available.
- The flexibility makes it likely that attackers will not optimize attacks, but rather will tend to "satisfice" (i.e., settling for what is "good enough") in undertaking attacks, which protects them from having their plans seriously disrupted by information protection strategies.
- Attackers have certain advantages in terms of basic accessibility to U.S. targets that are very difficult to deny. They can also draw on widespread diffusion of technical knowledge about basic types of critical infrastructure, such as oil refineries or dams, to plug in data gaps even against facilities that are protected by typical kinds of perimeter security.
- Information protection strategies probably will not make much of a difference on their own, but such measures can serve as effective adjuncts to robust physical protection strategies and contribute to depth in the defensive strategy.

Summary

Our assessment of an attacker's information requirements suggests that geospatial information is probably not the first choice for fulfilling the attacker's information needs, given the degree of flexibility that attackers have in planning attacks on targets in the United States.

Although geospatial information is somewhat useful for helping with selecting a target and determining its location, it appears likely that possible attackers, such as terrorist groups or hostile governments, will desire more trustworthy information that they can obtain from direct access or observation. In addition, most attacks are likely to require very detailed information for attack planning purposes. This type of information, which mostly comes from such nongeospatial sources as engineering textbooks, technical publications, trade journals, or human expertise on the operations of a particular type of industrial complex, is essential for attackers to have a high confidence in satisfying the information requirements of the more demanding attack planning part of the targeting problem. The next chapter examines the sources of publicly available geospatial data and information that may be useful to an attacker and provides greater insight into alternative sources of publicly available geospatial information.

CHAPTER THREE

What Publicly Available Geospatial Information Is Significant to Potential Attackers' Needs?

In the preceding chapter, we focused on information "demand," or what information potential attackers might need to carry out an attack on U.S. critical infrastructure or other key locations.[1] In this chapter, we turn to the supply side to assess which types of geospatial information are publicly available and significant to fulfilling the information needs of adversaries planning an attack. Our analysis focused on two key questions: (1) What federal geospatial information is publicly available? and (2) How significant is it? For our purposes, we defined "significant" based on whether the information is both *useful* and *unique*. Our methodology consisted of three main parallel processes:

1. We conducted a structured survey to identify and assess publicly available geospatial information about critical sites at hundreds of federal data sources. The assessment process included sampling and analyzing more than 600 federal databases available from these federal sources.
2. We conducted interviews and group discussions with federal, state, and local security and geospatial data experts about sources of publicly accessible federal and nonfederal data and users of federal data. This process helped us to better appreciate the concerns,

---

[1] Throughout this chapter, U.S. critical infrastructure and other key locations are referred to by the term "critical sites."

41

issues, and insights that they had about identifying potentially sensitive geospatial information and consideration in restricting access to this information.

3. We also sampled and examined more than 300 nonfederal sources (e.g., state and local governments, private corporations, NGOs, and foreign sources) to understand the larger information context concerning the availability of these alternative information sources compared with federal geospatial information.

We discuss the methodology in greater detail throughout this chapter.

Federal Geospatial Information in the Public Domain

Any assessment of what publicly available federal geospatial information is significant must begin by identifying what types of geospatial information are made publicly available by federal agencies. To this end, we conducted a structured survey to sample and identify the range of federal geospatial data sources.

Structured Survey Used to Identify Federal Geospatial Data Sources

In this survey, we first sought to identify federal geospatial data sources—specifically, the programs, offices, and major initiatives that generate publicly accessible geospatial information. For example, the Department of Energy's (DOE's) Energy Information Administration (EIA) has an initiative to provide infrastructure maps for energy market and end home use for different regions of the country.[2] The initiative is a geospatial data source for U.S. energy infrastructure maps.

For our analysis, we assumed that any significant federal activity that makes geospatial information publicly available would most likely advertise the availability of such information through a public

---

[2] See www.eia.doe.gov/emeu/reps/states/maps/contents.html.

Web site, so we conducted a systematic Web-based search. This search was then supplemented by selected interviews and hard-copy document reviews. Our survey involved several person-months of effort, and we examined more than 5,000 federal Web sites.

Our search consisted of three main parts:

1. We conducted a structured hierarchical search of the Web sites of all major federal executive and independent agencies as well as the ones most likely to contain geospatial information about critical sites. We searched 69 federal agencies.[3] Starting at the main home page of each organization, we searched down through the sites to examine programs, offices, and main initiatives and to identify the ones that provide some sort of geospatial information. Figure 3.1 shows a simplified example of how we conducted this hierarchical search for part of DOE.

Given the fact that each agency has different organizational structures, approaches to providing Web information, and types and locations for providing geospatial information, we used four different methods to search systematically throughout each organization to identify as many significant sources as possible:

- We looked at each agency's organizational chart, and then searched each administrative link to programs, offices, and other subagencies' components that might contain geospatial information and then searched down through each of these branches to identify possible sources.
- We looked at what each agency does and searched parts of the agency that have functions related to critical infrastructure and/or geospatial information. For our search, "functions" referred to agency activities that were not clearly identified with the organizational parts of the agency. For example, DOE had a separate Web page where users could find energy efficiency information.

---

[3] For a full list of the agencies searched, see Appendix A.

Figure 3.1
Simplified Example of Hierarchical Search of Department of Energy Web Sites

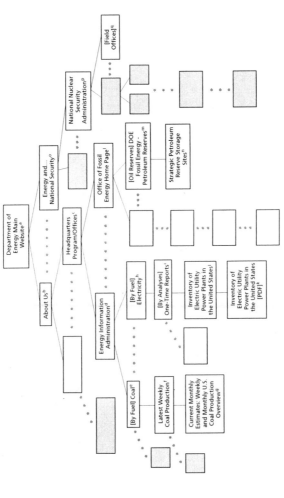

NOTE: Dots represent multiple horizontal and vertical levels that were searched.

RAND MG142-3.1

[a] http://www.energy.gov
[b] http://www.energy.gov/aboutus/index.html
[c] http://www.energy.gov
[d] http://www.eia.doe.gov/
[e] http://www.eia.doe.gov/cneaf/coal/fuelcoal.html
[f] http://www.eia.doe.gov/cneaf/coal/weekly/weekly_html/wcppage.html

[g] http://www.eia.doe.gov/cneaf/coal/weekly/weekly_html/wcpweek.html
[h] http://www.eia.doe.gov/fuelelectric.html
[i] http://www.eia.doe.gov/cneaf/electricity/page/pubs.html
[j] http://www.eia.doe.gov/cneaf/electricity/ipp/ipp_sum.html
[k] http://www.eia.doe.gov/cneaf/electricity/ipp/ipp99.pdf
[l] http://www.energy.gov/security/index.html

[m] http://www.dp.doe.gov
[n] http://www.nnsa.doe.gov/map.htm
[o] http://www.fe.doe.gov
[p] http://www.fe.doe.gov/program_reserves.html
[q] http://www.fe.doe.gov/spr/site_descriptions/spr_sites.html

- We searched the data warehouse Web sites at each agency.
- We searched agency press releases and news items to identify possible sources for critical site and geospatial information.

2. Next, we examined documents and Web sites describing federal agency geospatial information sources to check for additional agency locations that might provide publicly accessible geospatial information. Such sources included the Federal Geographic Data Committee (FGDC) Web sites and selected documents, such as the metadata warehouse and agency annual reports to the FGDC. Another example was the National Academy of Public Administration (NAPA) report, *Geographic Information for the 21st Century.*[4]

3. Finally, we carried out a key word search (using Google and other Internet search engines) to identify federal (as well as nonfederal[5]) Web sites. Key words related to critical infrastructure types and geospatial information were used in this search. Examples of such words and phrases include "NRC 'plant information book'"; "'public water supply' GIS"; and "sensitive infrastructure geospatial site:.gov".

In addition, we also searched libraries (such as a Government Printing Office depository library, a county library, and a university library) and reviewed our findings or had discussions with selected federal agency representatives (e.g., from NGA, EPA, FGDC, the Department of the Interior [DOI], the National Aeronautics and Space Administration [NASA]) to make certain we had identified the majority of federal geospatial data sources.

Since our definition of geospatial information was very broad, our survey included searches for textual documents that contained geospatial information, as well as such traditional geospatial sources as

---

[4] NAPA (1998).

[5] These nonfederal sites are discussed later in this document when describing the alternatives analysis.

geospatial data clearinghouses.[6] In addition to searching main federal programs and offices, we also focused on federal regional office and interagency activities, since they also are important federal geospatial information distributors.

As a result of our search, we found that publicly accessible federal geospatial information is spread across many agencies and activities within those organizations. In fact, we identified 465 programs, offices, or major initiatives[7] at 30 different federal agencies and departments that make various types of geospatial information publicly accessible. Table 3.1 shows how these sources break out by different federal agencies and departments. DOI has the largest number of geospatial information sources (22.2 percent of the federal total), followed by DOE (11.8 percent). However, since these numbers are a source count by programs and major activities, an agency-by-agency comparison can be misleading because the volume of data at any one source is not accounted for. For example, NASA and NOAA provide large amounts of publicly available geospatial information, but such information is available through a few main programs, while DOI has many different subagency organizations that provide geospatial information, including the Bureau of Land Management (BLM), the Bureau of Reclamation, the Fish and Wildlife Service, the Minerals Management Service (MMS), the National Park Service, and USGS. Nonetheless, this systematic survey was useful in identifying the range of publicly available sources of federal geospatial data and information that are the main focus of this study.

---

[6] A geospatial data clearinghouse is an organization that acquires, maintains, and distributes geospatial data or provides informational services about such data for many different data users. Such an organization may also integrate the data, generate the data, or perform other types of data-processing functions. Many federal agencies, states, and universities have been developing geospatial data clearinghouses.

[7] Appendix B contains a list of the Web sites for these many different sources.

Table 3.1
Number of Federal Geospatial Data Sources,[a]
Sorted by Agencies with the Highest Number of Sources

Agency Name	Number of Data Sources	Percentage of Total
Department of the Interior	103	22.2
Department of Energy	55	11.8
Department of Transportation	45	9.7
Environmental Protection Agency	43	9.2
Department of Agriculture	40	8.6
Department of Defense	34	7.3
Department of Commerce	29	6.2
Department of Health and Human Services	20	4.3
Interagency/other[b]	15	3.2
Department of Justice	11	2.4
National Aeronautics and Space Administration	11	2.4
Federal Emergency Management Agency	9	1.9
Nuclear Regulatory Commission	6	1.3
Tennessee Valley Authority	6	1.3
Department of the Treasury	6	1.3
Department of State	5	1.1
Federal Communications Commission	4	0.9
Department of Housing and Urban Development	3	0.6
General Services Administration	3	0.6
Library of Congress	3	0.6
National Science Foundation	3	0.6
Architect of the Capitol	2	0.4
Department of Labor	2	0.4
Central Intelligence Agency	1	0.2
Defense Nuclear Facilities Safety Board	1	0.2
Export-Import Bank	1	0.2
National Archives and Records Administration	1	0.2
Supreme Court of the United States	1	0.2
U.S. International Trade Commission	1	0.2
U.S. District Courts	1	0.2
Total	465	100

[a]A federal geospatial data source is any major federal program, office, or major initiative that provides publicly accessible geospatial information.
[b]Interagency/other refers to initiatives that are sponsored by multiple agencies.
NOTE: Percentages do not add exactly to 100 percent due to rounding.

Availability of Nonfederal Geospatial Information

As we were identifying federal geospatial data sources, we also conducted a sampling process to identify nonfederal geospatial data sources related to U.S. critical sites. While the main focus of this study was on *federal* sources, it is important to consider the broader context of alternative geospatial sources. After all, if many other nonfederal sources provide the same information, restricting access to the information at the federal agency level does not enhance security. The overall objective of this search of nonfederal sources was to understand how widespread and available the alternative sources or substitute information were for publicly available federal geospatial information on U.S. critical sites.

For our analysis, an *alternative source* refers to any other federal, state, and local government; commercial; academic; NGO; individual; or foreign information source in which similar information could be obtained. The actual alternative source could be in any form, including hard-copy maps, GIS datasets, video clips, photographs, Web sites, handheld GPS receivers at the site, and hard-copy documents.

Since our primary focus was on federal sources, our survey to identify and sample nonfederal sources was similar but less thorough. This systematic search involved visiting more than 2,000 nonfederal Web sites to identify and examine nonfederal activities that provide publicly accessible geospatial information; it also involved the identification of a sample of more than 300 nonfederal alternative sources. This search was not meant to be exhaustive but to sample alternatives selectively to understand the range of alternative sources and identify the ones most likely to contain sensitive geospatial information about U.S. critical sites. The survey consisted of four main parts:

1. **A key word search (using Google and other Internet search engines) to identify nonfederal Web sites.**[8] We used words and

---

[8] This search was conducted in parallel with the federal search using some of the same key words.

phrases related to critical infrastructure types and geospatial information, such as "nuclear 'plant information book'" and "'public water supply' GIS".

2. **A directed search of key geospatial data clearinghouses based on extensive knowledge of such clearinghouses from previous RAND work.** For example, in a study for NASA's Science Data Buy program, RAND analysts had examined and conducted case studies on more than 20 nonfederal geospatial clearinghouses.[9] Similarly, a RAND study for the Global Spatial Data Infrastructure examined more than 30 national and regional spatial data infrastructure activities.[10]

3. **Discussions with federal, state, and local governments about alternative sources and a review of the suggested sources.** This analysis included a teleconference and emails with the National States Geographic Information Council (NSGIC) homeland security working group (representing about 20 different states[11]) and group meetings with EPA and DOI geospatial information experts. In addition, we conducted telephone interviews with local government officials in diverse parts of the United States, including, for example, New York City and Teton County, Wyoming.

4. **A search for alternative information sources, including Web-based maps, documents, and other products, by looking for specific critical infrastructure types and sample critical sites.** For example, we asked: What information sources can we find on U.S. nuclear power plants? What information sources can we find on a particular nuclear plant (e.g., the Calvert Cliffs nuclear power plant in Maryland)? This search consisted of three different parts:

---

[9] See Pace et al. (2000, pp. 40–44 and Appendix 3).

[10] See Lachman et al. (2002).

[11] State representatives who participated in the conference call or provided input by email or through separate interviews included Arizona, Arkansas, California, Kansas, Kentucky, Maryland, Missouri, Montana, New York, North Carolina, Ohio, Oregon, Tennessee, Utah, Washington, West Virginia, and Wyoming.

- While conducting the targeting analysis and targeting case studies (Chapter Two), we identified alternative information sources for the selected targets.
- In examining and classifying the set of critical sites, such as nuclear power plants and chemical facilities, we searched for and identified information sources on such sites.
- In searching for alternatives for specific federal geospatial databases, we identified alternative sources for each database. This specific alternative analysis is discussed in more depth later in this chapter.

Diverse Range of Nonfederal Geospatial Sources

As a result of our search, we found a diverse set of alternative sources providing geospatial information on U.S. critical sites (as illustrated in Table 3.2). Such widespread availability of geospatial information is not surprising given our open society, the accessibility of many critical sites, and the importance of geospatial information to many different areas of American life. In fact, most business and government datasets have significant geographic content; it has been estimated that 75 percent of business data have some type of geospatial content.[12] Such information is needed for numerous public- and private-sector activities, including transportation of goods and services; understanding market conditions and demographics; analyzing environmental conditions; producing food; constructing, maintaining, and designing buildings, infrastructure, and communities; providing public safety and defense; etc.

To understand better why so many diverse alternative sources exist, we briefly discuss each source type: industry/commercial, universities/colleges, NGOs, state and local governments, international organizations, and individuals/private citizens.

---

[12] Frost & Sullivan (1999, p. 5-2).

Table 3.2
Examples of Nonfederal Geospatial Information Sources[a]

Type of Source/ Source Example	Example of Geospatial Information Provided by the Source	URL/ Product Type[b]
Industry/Commercial Businesses		
Pennwell Oil and Gas	Energy and infrastructure information, such as industry specific maps	www.mapsearch.com/ digital_products.cfm
AllTopo Maps	Commercial distribution for USGS topographic maps that contain information about roads, trails, etc.	CD-ROM
Thomas Brothers map books	The *Thomas Guide* provides detailed road maps of local areas across the United States	www.thomas.com
Sunoco Oil Company	Provides oil refinery information	www.sunocoinc.com/ aboutsunoco/ facmhook.htm
Microsoft Terraserver	DOQs showing 1-meter images of buildings and other surface features	terraserver.microsoft. com; www.maptech.com
Universities/Colleges		
University of California–Berkeley's REGIS program	Coastal area maps that include information about offshore oil platforms	www.regis.berkeley. edu/glinks/
Cornell University's Digital Earth	Geographic, geologic, geophysical, and imagery datasets, including images of potential critical sites	http://atlas.geo.cornell. edu/geoid/metadata. html
University of Arkansas Libraries On-Line Geospatial Data	Clearinghouse with links to major GIS holdings across the Internet—for example, hospital and airport GIS information	http://libinfo.uark.edu/ GIS/us.asp
University of New Mexico's Traffic Crash Data Center	Information about major nodes of concern for state transportation infrastructure	www.unm.edu/%7 Edgrint/tcd.html#gis

Table 3.2—Continued

Type of Source/ Source Example	Example of Geospatial Information Provided by the Source	URL/ Product Type
NGOs		
GlobalSecurity.org	Specific information related to U.S. military and government facilities	www.globalsecurity.org
Washington D.C. Suburban Sanitary Commission	Information regarding water and sewer pipe infrastructure	www.wssc.dst.md.us
Clary-Meuser Research Network	Information about chemical emissions from industrial plants	www.mapcruzin.com
Federation of American Scientists	Specific information related to U.S. nuclear and aerospace facilities	www.fas.org
National Academy of Engineers	Specific technical information related to U.S. industry and infrastructure	http://books.nap.edu/nap-cgi/srchnax.cgi?term=infrastructure
Natural Resources Defense Council: 1987 Nuclear Warhead Facility Profiles, Vol. III	Reference document providing technical facility and operational details related to U.S. nuclear sites	Hard-copy document (Cochran, 1987)
Environmental Defense: Scorecard.org	Information about chemical plants	www.scorecard.org
State and Local Governments		
Fairfax County, Va.	Parcel and other GIS datasets, for example, providing information about federal office buildings	www.co.fairfax.va.us/maps/map.htm
Teton County, Wyo. map server	GIS infrastructure and parcel maps showing roads and property ownership	www2.tetonwyo.org/mapserver/
Texas Natural Resources Information System	GIS base layers including energy, imagery, and transportation	www.tnris.state.tx.us/DigitalData/data_cat.htm

Table 3.2—Continued

Type of Source/ Source Example	Example of Geospatial Information Provided by the Source	URL/ Product Type
State and Local Governments (cont.)		
Montgomery County, Md.	GIS datasets providing information about schools and police beats	http://gis.montgomery countymd.gov/
New Jersey Department of Environmental Protection	Environmental and infrastructure datasets, including information about oil and chemical plants	www.state.nj.us/dep/gis/
San Diego Area's SanGIS	Transportation, water, and local infrastructure	www.sangis.org/sangis/intmaps/index.html
New York State GIS Clearinghouse	GIS datasets with infrastructure information	www.nysgis.state.ny.us
International Organizations		
International Commission on Large Dams/World Commission on Dams	Large repository of international data on dams and dam safety issues	www.icold-cigb.org/anglais.html www.dams.org/
International Atomic Energy Agency	International databases on major civilian nuclear power facilities, including U.S. facilities	www.iaea.org/worldatom/Reference/
International Association of Ports and Harbors	Information about ports and harbors	www.iaphworldports.org/link/main-link.htm
Saint Lawrence Seaway Binational Website	U.S. and Canadian facility infrastructure information	www.greatlakes-seaway.com/
Individuals/Private Citizens		
Computer Enthusiast	Maps of major Internet backbone nodes available for all major networks	www.nthelp.com/maps.htm
The Virtual Nuclear Tourist (.com)	Technical information regarding nuclear reactors	www.nucleartourist.com
Bicycling enthusiast's Web site	Internal photographs of major U.S. dam	www.theslowlane.com/93tripc/pumps.html

Table 3.2—Continued

Type of Source/ Source Example	Example of Geospatial Information Provided by the Source	URL/ Product Type
Individuals/Private Citizens (cont.)		
Scuba-diving enthusiast's Web site	Scuba-diving magazine details general swimming conditions around offshore facilities	www2.scubadiving.com/US/oilrigs/
Militaryliving.com	"Human interest" maps for retirees and military families of military installations	www.militaryliving.com/maps.html
Railroad enthusiast's Web page	Information about a U.S. critical site	home.earthlink.net/~southrail/page3.html

[a]We are not saying these sources do or do not provide sensitive information on U.S. critical site, but rather that they provide geospatial information on such sites.
[b]These Web sites were accurate and available during our research collection in 2002. Some of them may have changed or been removed since then.

Industry/Commercial. Given the myriad uses of geospatial information, there are many commercial sources that generate, possess, and sell geospatial information. In addition, since commercial companies own, build, operate, and/or maintain so many of U.S. critical sites, these companies and their industry trade groups have significant amounts of geospatial information that they make publicly accessible. Critical sites in which the private sector plays such a major role include transportation centers, energy transmission and supply, chemical facilities, dams, nuclear plants, and water supply and treatment plants. Moreover, private companies often are the original source of federal geospatial information because they provide some of their geospatial information to the federal government, given federal reporting requirements, or because they choose to sell it.

Universities/Colleges. For educational and research purposes, universities, colleges, and trade schools also provide the public with geospatial information available about U.S. critical sites. Students who are engineering, architecture, and management majors, for example, need to learn about public infrastructure to become the future builders, maintainers, and managers of such facilities. Real-world examples are an important part of these academic and trade professional education processes. Universities and colleges make such information readily available through their libraries and Internet sites. In addition, publicly sharing geospatial information related to critical sites can be important for research purposes, such as sharing findings and publishing peer-reviewed articles in technical journals. For example, earthquake and structural engineering researchers share information about structural design and experiences in designing bridges in earthquake-prone areas to facilitate more resistant structures.

Nongovernmental Organization Sources. Since many critical sites have safety and environmental concerns that can affect local communities, especially in the event of an accident or natural disaster, many community and NGO groups provide information about these sites. For example, diverse local, national, and international environmental groups make available information on facilities that use hazardous materials and nuclear plants. As cited in Table 3.2, an illustration of such a source is the Natural Resources Defense Council nuclear weapons manufacturing information book, which provides some detailed information about the location and operations of U.S. nuclear weapons complexes. These NGO groups see their role as making information about the sites as public as possible, educating communities about potential risks, and serving a watchdog role for these sites to ensure they are properly managed to address risks and community concerns. And since environmental, safety, and community right-to-know laws require public access to much geospatial information about many of the sites, these groups can legally acquire and distribute such information.

State and Local Government Sources. State and local governments use critical site geospatial information to improve their operations and the services that they supply to the public. For instance, they use geospatial information about such features as water systems, utilities, hazardous chemical sites, road systems, and property ownership to maintain, inspect, regulate, and operate community infrastructure and facilities; to prepare for emergency response, transportation, and other community planning; and for other purposes. As a result, they become significant suppliers of such information, sharing and making information readily available in the public domain. Indeed, state and local open records, laws, and policies may require such access. However, many governments share geospatial information for such benefits as reducing the expense and time required to collect, distribute, and use geospatial information, as well as to improve the overall quality of geospatial data and information for public-policy decisionmaking. In addition, some local governments, such as Fairfax County, Virginia, sell their geospatial data to the public to help pay for the costs of creating and maintaining it.

International Sources. Given the current trend toward globalization and the ability to easily copy and provide information through the Internet, international sources containing geospatial information about U.S. critical sites also exist and are often readily available. These sources include technical and professional organizations, international trade associations, foreign companies, international NGOs, and even private individuals who post information on their Web pages.

Individuals/Private Citizens. Since private citizens visit actual critical sites or go near them for work, leisure activities, or simply because they live near them, they inevitably acquire geospatial-related knowledge about these sites. Because of the Internet, more and more private citizens are disclosing such information in the public domain. Sharing recreational and hobby information through personal Web pages and chat rooms are examples of why and how individuals can make geospatial information related to critical sites publicly available. For example, in our survey, we found a scuba-diving enthusiast's Web site that featured information about currents around an oil platform off the Santa Barbara coast (discussed in more detail below).

Nonfederal Geospatial Sources Derived from Federal Sources

Many nonfederal geospatial datasets, or parts of them, may have originally come from federal sources. For example, numerous commercial topographical map products have their origins in USGS maps. Similarly, some state and local GIS transportation datasets (e.g., those of detailed GIS street networks) may be derived from the U.S. Census Bureau's Topologically Integrated Geographic Encoding and Referencing system (TIGER) database. This database defines the location and relationship of streets, rivers, and railroads to each other and to geographic areas for which the Bureau tabulates data.

In examining alternatives for an individual dataset, especially if only few alternatives exist, it is important to consider, for two main reasons, whether the original source is federal. First, such examination can show how other organizations depend on federal geospatial information. Second, it can show that restricting public access may result in the elimination of an alternative source. However, if the geospatial information is already widely distributed, such as with USGS topographical maps and the TIGER database, then removing the information from public domain would not remove existing alternatives. As a consequence, concerns about nonfederal sources that may use federal sources is likely to be more of an issue for updated and new types of federal geospatial datasets. In addition, if there is enough nonfederal demand, then industry, state and local governments, or another entity may update or create its own version of the products, even if they do not have an ongoing federal source. For example, topographical maps and GIS street networks are so popular for commercial and local government applications that private vendors and local governments would likely create such products on their own; in some cases, they already do. Thomas Brothers has been creating, selling, and using its own digital street map products for more than 10 years and do not rely on TIGER or any other federal dataset. In turn, many state and local governments create more accurate GIS street network databases of their own—such as digitizing aerial images for the entire county—rather than relying on federal sources. In fact, the Census Bureau is now depending on some local governments to provide them with the basic GIS datasets for its TIGER database.

In discussions with state and local governments about their geospatial data for this study and in other RAND geospatial work,[13] we

---

[13] For example, in a study for the White House Office of Science and Technology Policy designed to explore the potential for a science-based indicator and information technology system to support collaborative natural resource management decisions, RAND developed a

observed that increasing numbers of state and local governments are producing, updating, and maintaining more of their own geospatial datasets without relying on federal sources as much as they did in the past. For example, local governments in urban areas like New York City, Los Angeles (city and county), and Washington, D.C. (and many of its suburbs) have their own detailed GIS databases, which prove useful for supporting government services—e.g., police, fire, and emergency medical services dispatching—and issuing building and environmental permits. Even governments in some rural areas, like Teton County, Wyoming, and nonurban counties in Maryland, have their own extensive GIS databases, which they maintain and update without relying on federal sources.

Given the information and geospatial technology advances of the past 10–20 years, such a trend makes sense. First, advances in the computer and broader information technology industry have helped bring down the cost of using geospatial systems and data. Data processing and computing power have increased significantly and also have decreased in price. Such changes have made the use of geospatial data and the processing of it—that is, investing in computer hardware and software—less expensive. Second, GIS software programs have evolved so that they have more capabilities and are easier and cheaper to use. Third, geospatial data are less expensive and simpler to acquire, create, and update. For example, GPS has made it easier to enter accurate geospatial coordinates from the field. Given all these reasons, and the fact that more state and local governments recognize the cost savings and other benefits of investing in GIS-based systems and geospatial data, it is not surprising that state and local governments are investing in their own geospatial data.

It is important to note that, since 9/11, some state and local governments are restricting public access to geospatial information, which may eliminate some alternative information sources. However,

---

prototype of a GIS-based indicator system that would support decisionmaking in the Greater Yellowstone Ecosystem. RAND researchers gathered and examined more than 600 diverse GIS datasets from more than 30 different sources, including diverse federal, state, and local government agencies; universities; NGOs; and private industry. Another RAND study example relates to geospatial data clearinghouses; see Pace et al. (2000).

which governments restrict and what they restrict appear to be inconsistent. In addition, many state and local governments have open records laws and policies requiring that geospatial information be publicly accessible. Such inconsistencies among nonfederal entities in restricting public access is another reason why a federal analytical process is needed to assess and identify potentially sensitive information by providing state and local governments a federal model that they can use in developing their own approaches.

Given such trends and the complexities of the diverse geospatial data sources, one cannot assume that restricting public access to a federal source will in turn eliminate the information being available from alternative sources, which may have been originally derived from the federal source. However, a full analysis of such trends and the original source of each nonfederal alternative are outside the scope of this study. The important issue here is that anyone considering restricting access to publicly available federal geospatial information should assess each dataset individually to understand the full implications of restricting access to parts of the dataset (including societal costs and whether there is any real impact on alternative sources) and to evaluate whether such restrictions actually enhance security.

This discussion illustrates how complex it can be to identify and analyze alternatives to an individual dataset and why an analytical process, as outlined in the next chapter, is needed to examine datasets individually, rather than making general judgments about all datasets at a given geospatial source. As such, we now return to the federal sources identified during our search.

Assessing Whether Sources Contain Potentially Critical Site Information

Once we identified federal sources for publicly available geospatial information, as outlined earlier, we needed to determine whether they contained any critical site information that might look useful to a potential attacker's information needs. Therefore, we identified specific databases and datasets[14] at these sources that appeared as though they might contain some potentially critical site information useful to an attacker. This identification served as our first-cut estimate, independent of the targeting assessment.

Of these federal agency sources, we identified a sample of 629 databases and datasets that looked like they might contain some type of geospatially oriented critical site information.[15] Given that we were unable to examine every database in detail, we focused on identifying sample databases that contained the most useful geospatial information related to U.S. critical sites. Within these databases, we sought the most sensitive geospatial information available. For example, if the source contained satellite imagery, we selected an image of the highest resolution. If the source seemed to contain diverse datasets of potentially sensitive critical site information, we selected multiple datasets. In addition, if the source contained information about multiple types of critical sites (e.g., both energy and water) and a single dataset did not contain both types of sites, we selected multiple datasets.

To this end, we selected databases and categorized them based on what *type* of critical sites they might contain in terms of potentially useful information for attackers. Table 3.3 shows the total number of databases of each critical site category for all 629 publicly accessible federal databases examined. Since some databases had information for more than one critical type, there was a "multiple" category for those that contained information about more than one critical site category type. The federal agency databases that appeared to have the most relevant geospatial information were mostly energy

---

[14] A *dataset* refers to a single data file, Web page, or document containing geospatial information, while a *database* refers to an organized collection of datasets—that is, a set of data files. An example of a database is the National Atlas of the United States (see www.nationalatlas.gov), which contains population, water, species, land cover, boundary files, and many other datasets.

[15] For ease of discussion, we use the term database and dataset interchangeably, even though, in some cases, the item was technically a database or dataset.

Table 3.3
Total Federal Databases Examined by Critical Site Category

Critical Site Category	Number of Databases	Percentage of Total
Energy	114	18.1
Transportation	87	13.8
Water	79	12.6
Agricultural	72	11.4
Multiple	63	10.0
Toxics or hazardous materials	60	9.5
Emergency services	38	6.0
Cultural icons	29	4.6
Large population gatherings	28	4.5
Health	25	4.0
Banking and finance	15	2.4
Military installations	14	2.2
Communications	5	0.8

sites (18.1 percent), followed by transportation (13.8 percent) and water (12.6 percent). Ten percent of the databases contained information that might be useful for more than one site type.

We next examined the 629 databases to assess their content for "potentially useful" critical site information—namely, assessing how the information might be useful. This analysis was a first-cut estimate based on different potential attacker uses. Specifically, we considered whether the information might help an attacker select a site to target or plan an attack against that site. Because of different geospatial considerations, we distinguished between two issues in target-site selection:

- Which site would an attacker likely choose based on a potential effect?
- What is the general location of the site?

An example of geospatial information used to help choose a U.S. critical site would be that used to assess the possible consequences of attacking the site, especially compared with other sites. For example, an attacker might want to know that chemical plant X has more lethal and higher volumes of chemicals and a larger residential population nearby than chemical plant Y. Accessible information about a site location of use to an attacker could be a geolocation reference (i.e., latitude and longitude), a street address, or a map showing roads near the site.

At first glance, much of the information in these databases appears potentially relevant to attackers' information needs (see Figure 3.2). On initial inspection, 78.4 percent (493 databases) of these 629 federal geospatial databases appear to have the "potential" to contain useful critical site data. These initial estimates were made by RAND analysts, not considering actual attacker information needs. Specifically, these estimates were made by RAND's geospatial data experts before showing or discussing them with the targeting experts. Of these databases, most (68.7 percent, or 432 databases) appear to provide general location information. Another 17.3 percent (109 databases) looked potentially helpful in choosing a target. Only 13.2 percent (83 databases) appeared to have detailed geospatial information that might be valuable in planning the actual attack, and 21.6 percent looked as though they had no potential to contain any useful critical site information.[16] It is important to note that these estimates were made without any consideration given to actual attacker information needs—that is, without assessing the information "demand" of a potential attacker.

However, the real issue is assessing *how significant this information would be to a potential attacker*. For example, how important is a federal Web site that provides the address or map showing the location of a nuclear power plant when that same location is in almost any phone book or on a map bought at the local gas station? If the

---

[16] These numbers do not add up to 100 percent because a database may appear relevant for multiple purposes, such as choosing a target and providing location information.

Figure 3.2
**At First Glance, Most of the Federal Databases Potentially Contain
Critical Site Information**

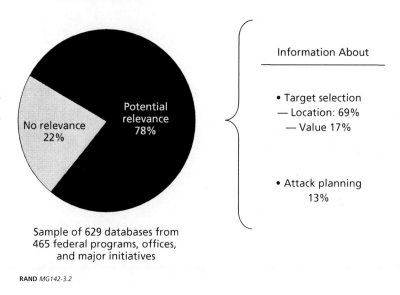

Information About

• Target selection
— Location: 69%
— Value 17%

• Attack planning
13%

No relevance
22%

Potential
relevance
78%

Sample of 629 databases from
465 federal programs, offices,
and major initiatives

RAND MG142-3.2

general location information for the critical site is such common knowledge and available from so many sources, it would not be significant. Once one factors in more detailed considerations as to the significance of the information available, the numbers presented here change drastically, as we see below.

Assessing the Potential Significance of This Information

The next step in our analysis was to assess whether this geospatial information was likely to be significant to an attacker's information needs. To perform such an analysis, we created a ranking estimate of the significance of the data based on the usefulness of the information and its uniqueness. Specifically, we used the following criteria:

1. How *useful* is the information to a potential attacker?

2. How *unique* is it? Namely, how many alternative sources are there for this information, or is even better information publicly available?
3. Given the usefulness and uniqueness of the information, is it *significant* for a potential attacker's information needs?

Assessing Potential Usefulness of the Geospatial Information

For our analysis, we estimated information usefulness based on the feedback from the targeting analysis, which ranked the usefulness of the information to the potential attacker. This classification was a rough estimate based on the targeting analysis, which assumed a range of potential attackers and attack modes (see Chapter Two). We ranked each database as either high, medium, low, very low, or none based on whether the information had the specific types of details and quality of information required to meet attackers' needs. *High* meant the geospatial information was critical information for the attacker—that is, the attacker could not perform the attack without this information. *Medium* meant the geospatial information could potentially be useful but was not necessary to complete the attack. *Low* meant the geospatial information probably was not likely to be useful but might be "nice to have"—that is, other, more pertinent information was probably more relevant, but this information may have a small chance of contributing to the attacker's general knowledge. *Very low* meant the information was not likely to have any usefulness or relevance to the attacker's information needs. *None* meant the geospatial information does not appear at all relevant to the attacker's expected information needs.

To classify each dataset, those of the RAND team focusing on "supply" (i.e., RAND federal geospatial analysts) met with those who had conducted the "demand," or targeting analysis (i.e., RAND targeting experts), and discussed what was in each dataset and how different potential attackers might use the information. Based on feedback from our targeting experts, our geospatial experts identified key features within each geospatial dataset that were deemed to have potential utility for either selecting a target or planning an attack.

This involved the entire team making a closer examination of these features and the role of this geospatial information for fulfilling the information needs of potential attackers on relevant U.S. critical sites. The RAND targeting experts provided the rankings based on their targeting analysis (see Chapter Two). In this assessment, the analysts took a fairly conservative approach, assuming something was more useful if there was any doubt, such as classifying something as *low* even though it seemed like there was only a very small or obscure chance that the information may be relevant to potential attackers. To illustrate this process, consider the U.S. EPA's Toxics Release Inventory (TRI). U.S. law requires EPA and the states to annually collect data on releases and other waste management activities of certain toxic chemicals from industrial facilities and to make them available to the public in the TRI. For the TRI, the targeting usefulness value was ranked *low* because, although its information about a facility may be nice to have and contribute to general knowledge, it would not be the first choice or most useful source of information for a potential attacker.

In our target assessment, we did not find any databases that would be ranked *high*. Namely, we could not find any publicly available geospatial information from federal agency sources that was considered critical for a potential attacker targeting U.S. critical sites. We did, however, identify 36 databases, or 5.7 percent of the total, that we ranked *medium* because they appeared as though they could potentially be useful to an attacker. We ranked another 205 databases, or 32.6 percent of the total, as *low* because of the small chance that they may contribute to attackers' general knowledge. Therefore, only 5.7 percent of the databases (the *medium* ranking) provided specific information that appear useful to attackers' needs (see Figure 3.3).[17]

---

[17] These datasets come from 6 percent of the federal sources, so we estimate that 94 percent of the federal geospatial data sources do not provide information that is particularly useful to an attacker.

Figure 3.3
Only 6 Percent of the Sample Provide Potentially Useful
Information

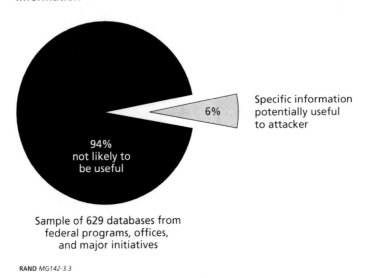

RAND *MG142-3.3*

Of these 36 databases that constitute the 5.7 percent *medium* risk category, 85.1 percent appeared useful for locating the target, 26.6 percent useful for selecting a target, and 21.6 percent useful for planning the attack.[18] Most of the useful information seemed more relevant for providing general location information. Of course, this type of information may be readily available from other sources, which leads to the next step in the analysis, assessing the *uniqueness* of this information by considering its availability through alternative sources.

Assessing the Uniqueness of the Geospatial Information

Next, based on our ongoing alternative source analysis, for the database elements of most concern, we examined how widespread and available the alternative sources and substitute information were. As

---

[18] These numbers do not add up to 100 percent because a database may appear relevant for multiple purposes, such as choosing a target and providing location information.

noted earlier, "alternative source" refers to any other federal, state, or local government; commercial; academic; NGO; individual; or foreign information source from which geospatial information could be obtained. Again, as discussed earlier, the alternative source could be in any form, including hard-copy documents and maps, GIS datasets, video clips, photographs, Web sites, and handheld GPS receivers at the site. This analysis provided insights on whether federal sources provide relatively unique geospatial information or whether comparable information is readily available from other sources.

For all federal databases in this study (i.e., each of the 629 sample databases),[19] we ranked alternative availability as *high, medium, low,* or *none.* We based this assessment on analyzing alternatives that are in a standard data format, such as a GIS dataset or Microsoft Excel data table, or a nonformatted data source, such as an industry trade journal or ease of direct access at the site. The first category we call an *in-class* alternative—i.e., a formatted data source. The second category we call an *out-of-class* alternative—i.e., a nonformatted, nontraditional source of geospatial data. The actual assessment process for ranking alternatives was based on the alternative analysis process discussed earlier in this chapter (see section on the availability of nonfederal geospatial information above). It also included searches to identify alternative sources for individual federal databases, and group discussions about each database by the RAND targeting and geospatial data experts to identify both in-class and out-of-class alternatives.[20]

---

[19] We looked more in depth at the federal databases that had any potential relevance to attackers' information needs (i.e., ranked high, medium, or even low for utility). There were 241 such databases. For each of these databases, we considered what piece(s) of information might be potentially useful to an attacker and what alternatives existed for this specific information.

Technically, if we had focused on databases that seemed relevant, we would have used only the high and medium databases to more thoroughly explore and assess alternatives. However, since there were only 36 such databases, this seemed too small a sample, so we chose to go with a more conservative approach and include the lows, resulting in a sample size of 241 databases.

[20] For each database, RAND analysts met, discussed, and described the alternatives to collectively rank them. If there were any questions about the availability of alternatives for a given

As part of this alternative analysis process, we conducted 11 in-depth case studies to identify specific alternative sources for the *same, similar,* and *additional information* for a specific critical site contained within a federal database, such as the Marcus Hook oil refinery plant in Pennsylvania for the TRI database. We discuss these case studies, including Marcus Hook, in more detail later in this chapter.

First, we ranked the databases for both in-class and out-of-class alternatives with values of *high, medium, low,* and *none* to indicate the potential volume of alternatives available. Then we created an aggregate alternatives value based on these two rankings.

A *high* alternative value means that the equivalent information is available from many sources, it is easy to re-create the information, and, in many cases, the information can be easily acquired by direct observation. For example, TRI was ranked *high* for alternatives because there are many sources for the same, similar, and even more useful information, compared with what is provided by this federal database. (Samples of these alternatives are presented later in this chapter; see, for example, Table 3.6.) For many critical sites, the general location information falls in this *high* category because the information is available in road maps, in phone books, and on multiple Web sites.

A *low* alternative value means that there are only a few alternative sources for the information, the information is not readily accessible by direct observation, and it is not easy to re-create the information. A good example in which there are few alternative sources is the detailed technical information about nuclear plant site layout and the key functioning components within the plant. We were able only to identify a few sources for such information.

Finally, a *medium* value means that there are some alternative sources for the information, it takes a higher level of analysis to derive or access the information, and direct observation is not as easy, even if public access is not completely restricted.

---

dataset, we conducted additional Web and literature searches for alternatives and held additional group discussions.

Assessing the Significance

Given these findings regarding the availability of certain information via alternative means, we turned to our final step: ranking the potential *significance* of the various federal databases based on a combination of the measures of *usefulness* and *uniqueness*. This combined estimate was a rough ranking of each dataset's significance in terms of potentially fulfilling the information needs of possible attackers. Based on a simple formula that combined the two measures, significance values were *high, medium, low, very low,* or *none.* This formula ranked datasets as less significant if they had higher alternative values—that is, if there were many alternative sources available for the information. Datasets ranked *low* to *none* for likely alternatives were considered to have higher significance than those with many alternatives. For example, if a dataset was ranked *medium* for targeting and *medium* for alternatives, it received a *low* rank in terms of significance because substantial alternatives were available for this piece of information. Similarly, a dataset ranked *low* for targeting and *low* for alternatives was considered *low* for significance. To illustrate this process, consider the TRI database: Since it was ranked *low* on usefulness and *high* for alternatives, it was ranked *very low* in terms of significance.

High significance means that some portion of the geospatial database likely needs some form of public access restriction. *Medium* significance means the database should be examined more closely because limiting public access to sensitive parts might result in enhancing homeland security. Such an examination should address all the pros and cons of possible restriction. *Low* significance means a database probably does not warrant restriction but should be more thoroughly examined based on the criteria outlined in Chapter Four. Databases ranked as *very low* or *none* are probably not significant for addressing attackers' information needs and do not warrant any type of public restriction. Ultimately, however, since our categorization process was a rough estimate, all the factors discussed in Chapter Four should be considered before restricting access to any part of a particular database.

Of the 629 federal databases examined, we found no databases to have a *high* level of significance, and only 0.6 percent (four databases from three different federal sources) were ranked as having *medium* significance. Another 10.5 percent (66 databases) of the total databases were ranked as *low* significance. The rest, 88.9 percent of the total, were ranked *very low* to *none*.

Therefore, we estimate that *fewer than 1 percent of federal data are both unique to federal sources and potentially useful to attackers' information needs,* compared with about 6 percent that is potentially useful to the attacker and about 94 percent that our assessment found to have no usefulness or low usefulness (see Figure 3.4).

Given these results, we conclude that only a few of federal agency geospatial sources appear significant to attackers' needs. However, we cannot conclude that federal information provides no special benefit to the attacker. Neither can we conclude that it would benefit the attacker. Our sample suggests merely that publicly available federal

Figure 3.4
Fewer Than 1 Percent of Federal Databases Appear Potentially Useful and Unique

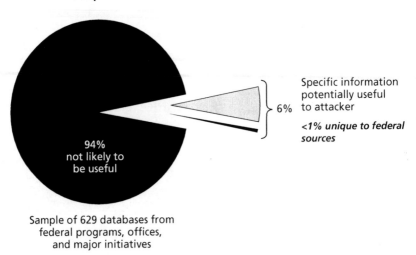

Specific information potentially useful to attacker

<1% unique to federal sources

6%

94% not likely to be useful

Sample of 629 databases from federal programs, offices, and major initiatives

geospatial information of potential homeland security concern, if it exists, is not scattered widely and may be scarce.

We might also add that the four *medium* significance databases have either been withdrawn since 9/11 or now include password protection to limit public access. In fact, we were unable to examine two of these datasets because of password restrictions; however, we found earlier versions of one of the others on an archive Web site. All four were a subset of 39 federal geospatial datasets that we identified as withdrawn from public view or offline since 9/11. Of the other 35 withdrawn datasets, which we found either on archive Web sites or detailed descriptions of their contents, none received a *medium* or *high* ranking in terms of their significance, suggesting these restrictions need to be more thoroughly assessed.[21]

A Closer Examination of the Potentially Significant Federal Databases

Our next step was to examine the *medium* and *low* significance databases (i.e., 11.3 percent of the total) to understand better how they were potentially relevant to attackers' information needs.[22] Of these databases, 80.0 percent (56 databases) appeared useful for locating the target, 30.0 percent (21 databases) for selecting a target, and 32.9 percent (23 databases) for planning the attack.[23] Thus, the databases have the most usefulness for potential attackers in terms of selecting the target, with most of these datasets providing general location information, which is not that useful for attackers. A small number of

---

[21] The decision of various federal agencies to restrict public access to these geospatial datasets that earlier had been publicly accessible may have been a prudent step in the aftermath of the 9/11 attacks. However, the relatively low ranking that these 35 datasets received in our assessment suggests that the responsible federal agencies should reexamine the public-access question with attention to some of the broader issues raised in this study (see Chapter Four) as a way of determining whether public access could be permitted to all or some portion of these datasets.

[22] Note that we included the low significance datasets in this examination to be conservative and to have a larger sample size.

[23] These numbers do not add up to 100 percent because a database may appear relevant for multiple purposes, such as choosing a target and providing location information.

databases appear to have limited usefulness in choosing a target, and slightly more appear to be significant for addressing the detailed information needs of planning an attack.

In our analysis, we also found that many of these medium and low significance databases were analytic tools rather than standard geospatial databases.[24] An analytic tool is a geospatial source that allows the user to analyze site information to help in comparisons and assessments of a site or multiple sites. Often such tools integrate diverse information so that someone can easily learn about the site. In fact, about 40 percent of the medium and low significance datasets (and 36.1 percent of the useful datasets—i.e., medium targeting values) consisted of such tools. Such datasets may help attackers choose a target more optimally because the data source provides a higher-level analysis capability. However, most of these analytic tools could also be duplicated with some simple analyses gleaned from other sources.

An example of such a tool is a Web site that contains information about multiple energy production or transmission facilities that the user can easily search for to assess the diverse time and spatial dimensions of energy volumes at the facilities. Many of these Web sites were also interactive, integrating different geospatial information into an easy-to-use tool. For example, the Department of Housing and Urban Development (HUD) has a Web tool, the Healthy Communities Environmental Mapping Initiative (E-MAPS[25]), that allows communities to view relationships between people and hazardous substances at different facilities. This public site combines other federal datasets, such as the Census Bureau's population and TIGER data with EPA's TRI database. In our analysis, E-MAPS was not found to be a significant database because it contains such general information that its usefulness is *low*. And because there are so many alternative sources with similar or better information, its uniqueness is also *low*. E-MAPS, however, does serve as a model to illustrate an

---

[24] Note that, within our analysis approach, we referred to and counted such sites as databases.

[25] Environmental Maps.

analysis tool. Such Web tools appear as though they could be potentially useful for attackers to choose a target more optimally. For example, with systems like E-MAPS that contain more detailed information, the user can look at populations near different toxic chemical facilities and compare the number of people and types of chemicals emitted to assess the effect of attacking each facility. Still, further analysis is needed to assess how valuable some of these tools are, especially given the fact that there is not compelling evidence that attackers try to choose the optimal target (see Chapter Two).

Case Studies Comparing Federal and Nonfederal Sources of Geospatial Information

We have already discussed how we searched for alternative sources of geospatial information, as well as the range and importance of the alternatives. Here we present specific in-depth case study examples to show specific substitute sources for information and how they compared with the federal sources. We also explain how we assessed the potential significance of the information at these federal sources.

We examined 11 diverse federal datasets as in-depth case studies based on sample critical sites (e.g., a specific local plant, dam, or bridge) for which federal databases provided information. We selected the cases to cover a range of geospatial information types (e.g., DOQ image, a map, textual documents containing geospatial information) and potential target types (e.g., dam, nuclear facility, military base, energy facility, ammunition plant) with an emphasis on what was viewed as more sensitive sites and information types. For example, DOI representatives were concerned about the public accessibility of inundation maps, and therefore we chose one as a case study. We also tried to complement what was already being studied in the targeting assessment—i.e., the demand analysis. For example, the demand analysis substantially investigated a possible attack on a liquefied natural gas facility, so we did not include this same type of facility in these cases.

The case studies included the following:

- DOI Bureau of Reclamation's DataWeb: Grand Coulee Dam
- DOI MMS: Houchin offshore mining platform
- HUD: E-MAPS/Marcus Hook oil refinery[26]
- NOAA nautical charts: Calvert Cliffs, Maryland, nuclear plant
- Nuclear Regulatory Commission (NRC) non-power/research reactors
- Tennessee Valley Authority: Environmental Impact Statement for Brown's Ferry nuclear plant
- U.S. Army Corps of Engineers: Los Angeles Reservoir Dam inundation maps
- U.S. EPA Biennial Reporting System (BRS): Milan, Tennessee, Army Ammunition Plant
- U.S. EPA's TRI: Marcus Hook oil refinery
- USGS: DOQ/MacDill Air Force Base, Florida
- USGS: topographic maps for different infrastructure at Grand Teton National Park and Yellowstone National Park.

For all these cases, we focused on identifying alternatives to the geospatial information that seemed to have the greatest possible use value for an attacker. For each case study, we answered the following questions:

1. What geospatial information does the source provide that could potentially be used by an attacker in choosing and planning an attack on the critical site?
2. What are the in-class and out-of-class alternatives for the *same, similar,* or *even more useful* information, and how easy is it to acquire such information from them?

---

[26] We explored the Marcus Hook facility for two different federal databases—HUD E-MAPS and EPA TRI—to examine the relationships between different federal sources that provide the same information. Namely, E-MAPS uses TRI data and combines it with other information, potentially adding more value to it, such as providing additional analytical capability.

3. Why is the information publicly available? Who uses it, and what is the public benefit?
4. Using our criteria, what is the significance of this information to meeting an attacker's potential information needs?

To illustrate this analysis, we discuss two examples that were not considered significant.[27] First, we look at a Web site containing the DOI MMS registry of offshore mining platforms. Then we discuss EPA's TRI, which is available in multiple formats and from multiple sources. We chose these two examples to illustrate the types of issues encountered in the analysis, such as the diversity of alternatives and how widely diffused public information can become.

DOI Minerals Management Service: Houchin Offshore Mining Platform Case Study

The MMS Pacific Region is tasked with overseeing the oil and gas operations and activities on leased areas of the federal outer continental shelf in waters near Southern California. Regulatory requirements govern the activities on these leases, providing for safe and environmentally sound operations. The MMS maintains a Web-based registry of offshore mining platforms in federal Pacific coastal waters: the DOI MMS Pacific Platform Operations Web site. At this data source, we chose to examine geospatial information about one specific site, the Houchin platform. The Web pages for this platform[28] provide general geospatial information about the platform and pipeline locations, including an image of the platform and a locational map showing the platform (see Figure 3.5, which depicts the map).

---

[27] Because of the sensitive nature of this information, we chose to discuss two nonsignificant examples to illustrate the issues. However, Appendix C contains information about the additional case studies, including information about the four databases that we ranked as medium significance.

[28] See www.mms.gov/omm/pacific/offshore/platforms/pacificopsplatform.htm#PLAT FORM%20HOUCHIN, and www.mms.gov/omm/pacific/images/sb.gif.

Figure 3.5
Map from Minerals Management Service's Web Site
Showing the Location of the Houchin Platform

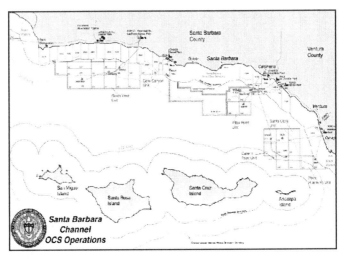

SOURCE: MMS, www.mms.gov/omm/pacific/images/sb.gif.
RAND MG142-3.5

One Web page also provides a text description that includes basic attribute information about the site, such as geospatial information. For example, the site notes that the platform is located at 4.1 miles off the California coast and at a water depth of 163 feet. This information is used by both the operators of the leases and others who are interested in the safety and guidance for sound operating practice at these sites.

Alternative sources describing the platform are readily available. In fact, there are many nonfederal sources with the same and potentially more useful information. Table 3.4 provides examples of these nonfederal sources. There are four types of information illustrated in this table: the image of the facility, the location of the facility, water depth, and energy production information. All these examples consist of general information that appears to be useful for a potential attacker in choosing the target and providing its general location.

Table 3.4
Federal and Nonfederal Data Source Comparison for the Minerals Management Service: Houchin Offshore Mining Platform

Data Element at Federal Site[a]	Nonfederal Alternative Sources Providing the Same Data	Web Address
Image of the facility	County of Santa Barbara Planning and Development: Energy Division	www.countyofsb.org/energy/ information/offshorePlatforms. asp
	Scuba Diving magazine	www2.scubadiving.com/US/oilrigs/
General location: 4.1 miles off the California coast	Maptech Nautical Charts	http://mapserver.maptech.com/ homepage/index.cfm?lat=34.3988 90000000002&lon=-119.5175& scale=232188&zoom=50&type=0& icon=0&searchscope=dom& scriptfile=http://mapserver. maptech.com/homepage/index. cfm&latlontype=DMS
	County of Santa Barbara Planning and Development: Energy Division	www.countyofsb.org/energy/ information/offshorePlatforms. asp
	California State Lands Commission Registry of Oil Platforms	www.slc.ca.gov/Division_Pages/ MRM/oilfacilities.htm
Water depth: 163 feet	Maptech Nautical Charts	http://mapserver.maptech.com/ homepage/index.cfm?lat=34. 398890000000002&lon=-119. 5175&scale=232188&zoom=50& type=0&icon=0&searchscope= dom&scriptfile=http://mapserver. maptech.com/homepage/index. cfm&latlontype=DMS
	County of Santa Barbara Planning and Development: Energy Division	www.countyofsb.org/energy/ information/offshorePlatforms. asp
	California State Lands Commission Registry of Oil Platforms	www.slc.ca.gov/Division_Pages/ MRM/oilfacilities.htm
	University of California Study on Decommissioning Platforms	www.ucop.edu/research/ucmc_ decommissioning/pdf/decomm_ report.pdf

Table 3.4—Continued

Data Element at Federal Site[a]	Nonfederal Alternative Sources Providing the Same Data	Web Address
Average Volume/Production: 808k/28M Avg Annl/Cum BBLS (average annual cumulative billion barrels)	S. L. Ross Environmental Research Ltd.	www.slross.com/publications/ mms%5C413-AssessmentOf DispersantsForCaliforniaAbstract. pdf

[a]www.mms.gov/omm/pacific/offshore/platforms/pacificopsplatform.htm#PLATFORM% 20HOUCHIN.

Alternatives for General Location Information. In terms of location information about the platform and pipelines, other federal sources offer the same type of information (e.g., nautical charts generated by NGA and NOAA). Some commercial coastal maps also provide such information. For example, Maptech sells a nautical chart for the area and provides a sample chart via the Web (see, for example, Figure 3.6).

Maptech's digital charts come from a federal source, NOAA. The company has a Cooperative Research and Development Agreement with the agency to produce such charts. Another source example is the County of Santa Barbara's Planning and Development Department's Energy Division,[29] which also supplies a coastal map showing the platform (see Figure 3.7).

Comparing Figures 3.5, 3.6, and 3.7, it is clear that all three maps contain basic information about the general platform location and pipelines going to shore. Such information needs to be on the nautical charts so that commercial ships and recreational boats do not collide with these sites. Given this need, such charts are widely available and easy to access or purchase without any accountability of who has acquired them.

---

[29] See www.countyofsb.org/energy/who/oil&gasMap.asp.

Figure 3.6
Maptech Nautical Chart Showing the Location of
Houchin Platform

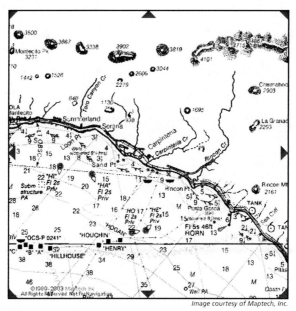

Image courtesy of Maptech, Inc.

RAND *MG142-3.6*

In addition, other federal agencies also provide locational information for Houchin. For example, USGS provides well information with latitudes and longitudes for the core drilling locations.[30] Because of environmental permitting requirements, EPA also supplies some basic location information on this platform.[31]

---

[30] See http://greenwood.cr.usgs.gov/crc/data/CA/ca-cotrs.htm.

[31] See www.epa.gov/region09/water/npdes/generalpermit1.pdf.

Figure 3.7
Santa Barbara County Map Showing the Location of Houchin Platform

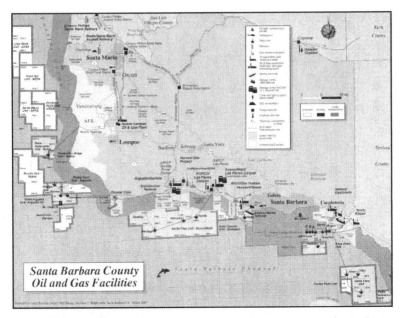

SOURCE: County of Santa Barbara, www.countyofsb.org/energy/information/
offshorePlatforms.asp.

RAND MG142-3.7

Sample of State and Local Government Sources. Similarly, state
and local governments supply information about the Houchin platform site for environmental and development permits and approval
processes. For example, the Santa Barbara County Air Pollution
Control District[32] provides detailed information regarding the facility
and its hazardous air quality emissions as required by law, namely
because of the facility's operating permit that is required by Title V of
the Clean Air Act Amendments. The county's Planning and Development Department supplies information about water depth and
location of the platform,[33] as do some state agencies, such as the Cali-

---

[32] See www.sbcapcd.org/eng/titlev/pooi.htm.

[33] See www.countyofsb.org/energy/information/offshorePlatforms.asp.

fornia State Lands Commission Registry of Oil Platforms.[34] This type of information is placed in the public domain because of public accountability for such facilities and/or state and local requirements or policies about public input or right to know.

Sample of Industry and Trade Association Sources. Rigzone[35] is a private company that supplies information about the oil and gas industry. It sells a digital three-dimensional marine chart that contains some locational information about the Houchin site. The Western States Petroleum Association, an industry trade group, also supplies minimal general information about the site.[36] Such groups as S. L. Ross Environmental Research Ltd.[37] often supply information about production at site, which provides the same average volume information as the MMS federal site (see Table 3.4).

Sample of Other Sources with Potentially More Useful Information. We also identified some unusual sources that provide potentially more useful information to attackers because they offer more specific information about the platform operational details and internal facility layout. We present three examples, which are detailed below and summarized in Table 3.5.

1. An online scuba-diving magazine contains a scuba diving enthusiast's article describing the swimming conditions around the platform, such as depth and surge. Such information could potentially be used by a scuba-diving attacker to estimate the accessibility of the platform.
2. A geologist tour group around the facility provides information that could potentially help more in planning an attack. For example, it provides more detailed pictures of the platform.

---

[34] See www.slc.ca.gov/Division_Pages/MRM/oilfacilities.htm.

[35] See www.rigzone.com/search/c/companies/exploration_production/.

[36] See http://api-ec.api.org/newsplashpage/index.cfm.

[37] See www.slross.com/publications/mms%5C413-AssessmentOfDispersantsForCalifornia Abstract.pdf.

Table 3.5
Examples of Nonfederal Data Sources Providing Additional Information on the Houchin Offshore Mining Platform

Type of Information	Nonfederal Alternative Source Description	Web Address
Estimate of platform accessibility by scuba diving	*Scuba Diving* magazine	www2.scubadiving.com/US/oilrigs/
Expert knowledge and detailed photos	Geologist tour group of the Houchin platform	www.geocities.com/Yosemite/ Meadows/5926/field.htm
Internal video of different parts of the platform	Television episode	www.thex-files.com/episodes/ season8/8x18.html

3. Video images of the actual site are available from tapes of a television episode. The entire episode takes place on the platform and contains detailed images of multiple locations on the platform.

All these examples illustrate the diversity of sources for similar, additional, and potentially even more useful geospatial information on the Houchin platform. Our sampling analysis found this pattern repeated in the other case studies. The details vary, but the fact that unexpected and unusual sources of information were found was common.

Ranking of the Significance of This MMS Information Source. We do not consider MMS a significant federal source for fulfilling an attacker's information needs for two reasons: its usefulness is low, and its information is not unique. The usefulness of this database (based on the targeting analysis) is ranked *low* because its information is so general, although it may increase potential attackers' "nice to have" knowledge about the site. It does little to reduce the need for the attacker to gather current, high-fidelity information that is necessary for detailed planning of an attack. In addition, since we found that many alternatives exist for this data source, as noted earlier, an attacker can readily obtain the same, similar, and potentially more useful information from other sources.

The Environmental Protection Agency's Toxics Release Inventory: Marcus Hook Facility Case Study

The federal Emergency Planning and Community Right-to-Know Act gives citizens the right to know about toxic chemicals being released into their communities. Sections 311 and 312 of the law require facilities in certain industries—facilities that manufacture, process, or use significant amounts of toxic chemicals—to report the locations and quantities of chemicals stored on-site to state and local governments to help communities prepare for chemical spills and similar emergencies. Section 312 of the law also requires EPA and the states to annually collect data on releases and other waste management activities of certain toxic chemicals from industrial facilities and make the data available to the public in the TRI. EPA compiles the TRI data each year, maintains the information in a multiyear database, and makes it available to the public on the Internet,[38] in compact disk format, and in written reports. EPA has several data access tools for this information, including the TRI Explorer and Envirofacts.

Benefits of Public Access to TRI Data. It is important to note the public benefit of TRI data. First, it has helped communities better prepare for possible emergencies. Second, since industries are required by law to submit detailed tracking information, it has helped industries to understand and track hazardous chemicals at their facilities more effectively and to motivate them to reduce their use and emissions of such chemicals because of the public visibility of such information. Third, environmental and community watchdog groups have used this information to help put pressure on facilities to reduce their use and emissions of such chemicals and to improve local emergency preparedness. In fact, it is well known in the pollution prevention field that public TRI declarations have helped motivate many companies to implement more pollution prevention activities.

---

[38] www.epa.gov/tri.

Alternative Sources for TRI Information. To explore alternatives for a specific critical site, we chose to look at the Marcus Hook, Pennsylvania, petrochemical plant (www.epa.gov/tri/tridata/tri00/ index.htm). Alternative sources describing this plant are readily available. In fact, there are many sources with the same, similar, and possibly more useful information.

Table 3.6 provides examples of these alternative nonfederal sources across two types of information they provide: location of the facility and chemicals located at the facility. All the examples provide general information for identifying and locating the Marcus Hook oil refinery.

Duplication of TRI data. Other organizations also make TRI data available to the public through their own data access tools. Federal sources include HUD's E-MAPS[39] and the Department of Commerce's LANDVIEW.[40] NGO sources include Unison Institute's RTKNet[41] and Environmental Defense's "Scorecard" tools,[42] both of which stem from environmental watchdog organizations that try to make it even easier for the public to use the information. For example, Scorecard integrates TRI data with other environmental and demographic datasets into a single, easy-to-use Web site with access to more than 400 datasets. The user types in a state, local community, or zip code to learn quickly about environmental issues in his or her community. Scorecard also allows the user to rank and compare the pollution situation in different areas—that is, comparing counties within a state or across the country. In turn, Scorecard profiles 6,800 chemicals, making it easy for anyone to find out where chemicals are used and how hazardous they are.

---

[39] See www.hud.gov/offices/cio/emaps/index.cfm.

[40] See www.census.gov/geo/landview/.

[41] See http://d1.rtknet.org/tri/.

[42] See www.scorecard.org/general/tri/tri_gen.html.

Table 3.6
Marcus Hook Oil Refinery: Federal and Nonfederal Data Source Comparison for the Environmental Protection Agency's Toxics Release Inventory

Data Element at Federal Site	Nonfederal Alternative Source for the Same Data	Web Address
General plant location: plant address	PASDA (Pennsylvania Spatial Data Access)	www.pasda.psu.edu/summary. cgi/epa/epa-pa_tri.xml
	Verizon Superpages.com directory listing	http://yp111.superpages.com/ listings.phtml?SRC=&STYPE= S&PG=L&CB=&C=&N=sunoco& T=marcus+hook&S=PA&R=N& search=Find+It
	MapQuest.com	www.mapquest.com[a]
Chemicals contained at the plant	PASDA (Pennsylvania Spatial Data Access)	www.pasda.psu.edu/summary. cgi/epa/epa-pa_tri.xml
	Right-to-Know network databases	http://d1.rtknet.org/ern/
	National Safety Council	www.nsc.org/library/chemical/ xylenes.htm
	Clary-Meuser Research Network	www.mapcruzin.com/tri_2000_ maps/#pa
	Good Neighbor Project for Sustainable Communities (Envirolink)	http://gnp.enviroweb.org/hf1. htm

[a]See www.mapquest.com/directions/main.adp?go=1&do=nw&ct=NA&1y=US&1a=1200 +South+Hayes+St&1p=&1c=Arlington&1s=VA&1z=&1ah=&2y=US&2a=7+W+DELAWAR E+AVE&2p=&2c=Marcus+Hook&2s=PA&2z=&2ah=&lr=2&x=48&y=15.

It is important to note that states also receive TRI data, and many states place their own version of the TRI data in the public domain. Therefore, even if the federal government decides to restrict access to TRI, the same data could be publicly available from state sources.

Besides the TRI data being available from other sources, there are also other sources that provide the same, similar, or potentially more useful information about a critical site. We illustrate some of these other sources by organization types for the plant at Marcus Hook.

Sample of Other Federal Sources. Other federal sources, such as EPA's Biennial Reporting System, DOE's EIA, and the Security and Exchange Commission also provide information about the plant.

Sample of State and Local Government Sources. State and local agencies also provide information to the public about the Marcus Hook site. The Pennsylvania Department of Environmental Protection, for instance, supplies information about the chemicals contained at the plant (see Table 3.6).

Sample of Industry and Trade Association Sources. Current and historical plant owners, plant suppliers, and the American Chemistry Council (formerly the Chemical Manufacturers Association) all supply information about the Marcus Hook facility. For example, on its Web site, Sunoco Facilities Information[43] provides a picture, an address, the number of employees, and detailed information about the main petrochemicals produced at the plant, including general capacity processing information. Moreover, Platts Petrochemical Alert,[44] an industry trade association, makes available information about plant production capacity.

Sample of Other Sources Providing Potentially More Useful Information. We also found a few nonfederal sources that contained operational details and internal plant facility information, which is potentially more useful information given attackers' needs. Information about the facility's security procedures (such as the number of guards on-site and technology upgrades) appears in a publicly available security management magazine. An industry press release about oil tankers by the Sun Company features a diagram showing oil tanker docking locations at the plant. These examples illustrate the diversity of similar or possibly more useful information available for the site.

Ranking of the Significance of This Toxics Release Inventory Information Source. For potential attackers' information needs, the TRI database was found to be not significant, because of both useful-

---

[43] See www.aristechchem.com/products/refineries.htm.

[44] See www.platts.com/features/ethylene/namericaplants.shtml.

ness and uniqueness considerations. The targeting value was ranked *low* because the TRI information about a facility may be "nice to have" and contribute to general knowledge, but it was not the first choice or most useful source of information for a potential attacker. For example, the information lacks currency and the specificity needed to plan an attack. Since alternatives were extensive, the information was not considered unique.

The TRI example illustrates the complexities of federal database control and access issues. First, all the TRI data come from private-sector companies and is shared with states that also place it in the public domain. Second, federal law requires the data be in the public domain to provide important public benefits. Third, data in the public domain have been already copied, used, and made accessible by many different types of organizations, as the examples discussed above illustrate. Fourth, diverse alternative sources exist for similar or more useful information. Given all these factors, even if it seems reasonable or feasible (which it does not, given the *low* usefulness of the information, many alternatives, and federal laws requiring public access), it would be very difficult to effectively restrict public access to the type of information that TRI provides. It would also diminish the public good that comes from providing local community access to information that can significantly affect the well-being of citizens. In addition, such restriction would not enhance security, since the information provided by TRI would still be easy to obtain from other sources.

Other Observations About Publicly Accessible Federal Geospatial Information

Key Issues in Federal Agency Data Sources

By examining federal data sources and interviewing data experts, we distinguished some other important issues about identifying potentially sensitive, publicly accessible, federal geospatial information and how it is distributed.

First, federal data are widely diffused in the public domain by many different sources. Federal datasets are distributed by other federal agencies, federal regional offices, state governments, industry, and NGOs. TRI provides a clear example of how federal information is quickly diffused across diverse sources in our open society. These other organizations also make decisions about whether and how to distribute the federal information publicly.

We also found differences in regional office and key partners' data sources and policies. Federal regional offices tend to have their own data control and data policies, which headquarters offices may or may not be aware of.

Second, a large amount of federal data on critical sites actually is information aggregated from state and local governments and industry sources. For example, much of the energy infrastructure data from DOE and DOI MMS, transportation data from DOT, and toxic and hazardous waste information from EPA originates from state, local, and industry sources. This occurs because many of the critical sites are owned or operated by the private sector and because states and local governments have authority for inspecting, certifying, and regulating such sites.

States may continue to provide public access to data, even in cases in which the federal government decides to restrict public access. For instance, USGS decided to withdraw a drinking water source dataset from the public domain after 9/11, but we found that a few states still had the same information publicly available. Similarly, private companies often sell industry geospatial information for industry needs.

Also there are many instances in which federal agencies have special relationships with industry regarding critical site geospatial information. Since private companies own or operate much of the U.S. critical infrastructure, such as energy and chemical facilities, energy networks, and nuclear plants, they often need access to federal information. They may provide the information publicly or supply their own information. For example, energy industry companies and trade organizations, such as Pennwell, sell detailed information about energy industry facilities and networks for commercial purposes.

Because of extensive trends in recent years to outsource base support, even military installations are depending on private contractors for utilities and other infrastructure support. In addition, there are important economic relationships between federal agencies and private-sector companies. For instance, many USGS map products, such as topographic maps, are distributed by commercial vendors that depend on such products for their income.

Third, and perhaps most important, we found that there is a range of public benefits from such data remaining unrestricted (as discussed further in Chapter Four).

Over the course of our study, we also noticed dynamic access to some of the federal data and changing access policies. As an example, for selected federal databases, agencies changed whether and how data were to be accessed through the Web by, for instance, requiring password access when prior to that, access was totally anonymous.

Another observation about federal data sources was that we found that online federal databases were searchable by useful attributes, such as Standard Industrial Classification codes or zip codes, while with other databases, the user needed to know the site already, such as by name or address. Such search capabilities provide an additional analytic capability to help attackers identify potential targets within an area or determine which ones meet certain criteria.

Summary

Our federal geospatial information survey found that publicly available geospatial information is spread across a wide range of federal government agencies and offices. Many different agencies are major distributors of publicly available geospatial information. We identified 465 programs, offices, or major initiatives at 30 different federal agencies and departments that make various types of geospatial information publicly accessible.

Our analysis found that very few of the publicly accessible federal geospatial sources appear useful to meeting a potential attacker's information needs. Fewer than 6 percent of the 629 federal geospatial information datasets examined appeared as though they could be useful to a potential attacker. However, we found no publicly available federal geospatial datasets that we considered critical information to an attacker's information needs (i.e., those that the attacker could not perform the attack without).

Our analysis suggests that most publicly accessible federal geospatial information is unlikely to provide significant (i.e., useful and unique) information for satisfying attackers' information needs. We found no publicly available federal geospatial datasets that we would rank as high-significance for providing useful and unique information. Fewer than 1 percent of the 629 federal databases examined had medium significance, and, since 9/11, these information sources are no longer being made public by federal agencies. An additional 10.7 percent had low significance and, therefore, are not likely to be useful to attackers.

However, we cannot conclude that federal information provides no special benefit to the attacker. Conversely, neither can we determine that this information would benefit the attacker. Our sample simply suggests that the publicly available federal geospatial information of potential homeland security concern, if it exists, is not scattered widely and may be scarce.

Two main reasons account for why such a limited number of publicly available federal geospatial datasets is likely to be of interest to potential attackers. First, the United States is an open information society with many alternative sources of information. Many nonfederal sources offer similar or better information (e.g., industry, NGOs, state and local governments, universities, non-U.S. sources). Second, most federally sensitive information was not publicly accessible prior to 9/11 because of preexisting security concerns. In addition, some possibly sensitive information has been withdrawn since 9/11.

A few federal sources appear to have possible but limited usefulness for choosing the best target due to their analysis capabilities. However, such sources require further analysis and a full-impact assessment before considering any restrictions, since such restrictions may not enhance U.S. homeland security, especially if ready substitutes exist and if attackers are flexible and determined.

In addition, our analysis found, in many cases, diverse alternative geospatial and nongeospatial information sources exist for meeting the information needs of potential attackers. We identified and sampled more than 300 publicly available nonfederal geospatial information alternative sources that provide geospatial information on U.S. critical sites. Our sampling of nonfederal geospatial data sources suggests that the same, similar, or more useful geospatial information on U.S. critical sites is available from a diverse set of nonfederal sources, which include industry and commercial businesses, academic institutions, NGOs, state and local governments, international suppliers, and even private citizens who publish their own relevant materials on the World Wide Web. In addition, relevant nongeospatial information is also available from the direct access or direct observation available for most U.S. homeland locations.

CHAPTER FOUR

An Analytical Framework for Assessing the Homeland Security Implications of Publicly Accessible Geospatial Information

Our assessments of the demand and supply aspects of the problem highlight the fact that decisionmakers need to weigh disparate factors in assessing the potential homeland security sensitivity of publicly available geospatial information. Thus, decisions on whether and how to restrict public access to this information will significantly benefit from using an analytical process that is explicit and consistently applied among geospatial information distributors.

Such a framework for analysis could help decisionmakers in weighing an interrelated set of relevant criteria concerning the usefulness, availability, and societal benefits and costs of public access to geospatial information. However, using an analytical process is no guarantee of producing quick or definitive answers. Nonetheless, an explicit set of criteria provides a useful first step toward a more coherent and consistent approach to information protection involving public access to geospatial information—at least until a more formal model can be developed over the longer term.

In this chapter, we seek to take this first step. Specifically, we outline an analytical framework that uses multiple filters to assess the homeland security implications of publicly accessible geospatial information. In addition, the chapter examines the types of precedents that the federal government already possesses for providing conditional public access to potentially sensitive information. Finally, it discusses the long-term need for a more formal and comprehensive approach for protecting geospatial and other potentially sensitive information concerning U.S. critical infrastructure facilities and key homeland assets.

Framework for Analysis: An Overview

The previous chapters highlighted the complex and diverse nature of the demand and supply aspects of publicly available geospatial information concerning the U.S. critical sites. These analyses suggest that a "one size fits all" set of guidelines based on a single key consideration is inappropriate. This chapter builds on the earlier analyses in developing an analytical framework for assessing the homeland security implications of publicly accessible geospatial information. In particular, it presents a framework for assessing the potential homeland security sensitivity of geospatial data or information based on the following *analytical filters* that highlight the salient factors for decisionmakers' consideration:

- *Usefulness*: the potential usefulness of geospatial information for planning attacks on U.S. critical sites. Attackers require particular kinds of information to identify targets and plan attacks.
- *Uniqueness*: the uniqueness of federal geospatial information sources. If alternative sources are readily available, the net security benefits of restricting access to the information may be minimal to nonexistent.
- *Benefits and Costs*: the expected societal benefits and costs of restricting the information. The chief benefit of restricting public access to geospatial information should be to improve U.S. homeland security against an attack. However, any expected benefits must also be weighed against expected societal costs that are likely to emerge because of the many public and private sector uses of the data and information.

Taken in combination, U.S. decisionmakers can use these key factors as a filtering process (see Table 4.1) for focusing their atten-

Table 4.1
Framework for Analyzing the Homeland Security Sensitivity of Geospatial Data and Information Sources

Filter	Key Questions for Decisionmakers
Usefulness	• Is the information useful for target selection or location purposes? • Is the information useful for attack planning purposes?
Uniqueness	• Is the information readily available from other geospatial information sources? • Is the information available from direct observation or other nongeospatial information types?
Societal benefits and costs	• What are the expected security benefits of restricting public access to the source? • What are the expected societal costs of restricting public access to the source?

tion on the cases in which restricting potentially sensitive geospatial information sources is likely to have the desired effect of enhancing homeland security without incurring an unacceptable societal cost. These filters offer decisionmakers and analysts a more structured method for assessing the sensitivity of geospatial information. For individual geospatial datasets, decisionmakers could use the framework to help assess whether and how to restrict access to all or part of such information.

This proposed framework is a useful first step in moving toward a more structured process that can be uniformly and consistently applied. Thus, the framework serves as an interim decisionmaking tool for responding to the near-term analytical needs of U.S. decisionmakers until the federal government can develop a more formal and comprehensive model for information protection of U.S. critical sites over the longer term.

Framework for Analysis: Three Analytical Filters

Our framework consists of three filters that identify key considerations that decisionmakers should weigh in assessing the homeland security implications of publicly accessible geospatial information. The first filter focuses on assessing the potential *usefulness* of a particular type of geospatial data or information for meeting the attacker's key information needs. The subsequent filters help the decisionmaker in evaluating both the feasibility and desirability of restricting public access to the geospatial information in question. The second filter addresses the feasibility of restricting public access to certain types of geospatial information by assessing whether it comes from a relatively unique source or whether comparable information is widely available to potential attackers from multiple (geospatial or other) sources. The third filter frames the desirability issue by recognizing the potential trade-offs involved in restricting public access to geospatial information from federal sources. At least in a general sense, this filter raises the importance of weighing the societal benefits of improving homeland security compared with the potential societal costs of restricting access to information that could be used for various public- and private-sector purposes.

Filter 1: Assessing the Usefulness of Geospatial Information for Target Selection and Attack Planning

The first filter assesses the usefulness of the geospatial information source for potential attackers. This assessment must consider the value of the information for selecting a target or for supporting attack planning.

Target Selection and Location Information. Our analysis of the demand side of the equation in Chapter Two suggests that potential attackers against U.S. homeland locations and facilities are likely to have, in most cases, both diverse information requirements and substantial flexibility for satisfying their information needs, especially for choosing and locating potential targets. For example, everything from road maps to safety markers show the location of many critical sites. Information about the size and general importance of critical sites, which can be used to help choose a target, is also readily available. Geospatial information databases are only one type of information that potential attackers have at their disposal. Other information sources, such as direct observation or social engineering, could be better suited for satisfying their very specific information requirements for executing an attack with a high expectation of mission success. The types of needed information vary substantially with the attack mode under consideration. In addition, potential attackers would be able to offset information collection shortfalls by altering their attack plans or target selections. This basic diversity and flexibility in the attacker's information requirements needs to be a key consideration in any assessment to identify the homeland security sensitivity of a particular geospatial information source.

Attack Planning Information. Once attackers select a target, they need detailed and timely information for planning their attack operations. Table 4.2 identifies some of the most sensitive types of information that attackers are likely to seek in planning their operations, which include both geospatial information (e.g., internal facility layout and location of facility vulnerabilities) and nongeospatial information (e.g., essential engineering details or security personnel equipment). This table refers only to features that are not directly observable. This type of information is particularly valuable to attackers because it is not directly observable through either public access or overhead imaging. In addition, any information on the local or systemic consequences of achieving a successful attack, beyond the obvious impact, would probably be valued greatly by potential attackers. For example, up-to-date knowledge of the security measures and practices would not only be useful for the attackers' selection of targets but essential for planning an attack with high confidence. The values in the table represent our evaluation of the relative importance of the different types of high-value attack planning information when considered on a discrete basis. However, it does not preclude the possibility that any particular piece of information, whether geospatial or other, could have relatively higher value if the attacker is adept at aggregating the information in such a way to achieve a synergistic effect.

Table 4.2
Types of High-Value Attack Planning Information[a]

Examples of Sensitive Information Types	Target Selection	Attack Planning
Internal Features		
• Control centers		X
• Power sources		X
• Communication lines		X
Engineering Details		
• Facility construction	X	X
• Equipment layout and details		X
Operational Details		
• Day-to-day plant schedules	X	XX
• Security measures and practices	X	XX
Attack Assessment		
• Specific site consequences		X
• General impact (local or regional)	X	

[a]A single "X" indicates that a particular type of sensitive information is likely to be considered desirable in meeting attackers' information needs, while a double "X" indicates more highly desirable information.

Filter 2: Assessing the Uniqueness of Geospatial Information

The second filter in the analytical framework assesses whether a specific piece of geospatial information is available widely or only through federal sources. Any decision to restrict public access to such geospatial information needs to consider whether confining a particular piece of geospatial information would actually deny potential attackers needed information for executing an attack. This determination depends on whether the information provided by a geospatial source is relatively unique or whether information of comparable quality is readily available to the attackers from other sources. Such information could be publicly accessible geospatial information from nonfederal geospatial sources, as well as information that an attacker might obtain through direct reconnaissance of a potential target. If acceptable substitute sources of information are readily available, the expected homeland security benefits of restricting public access become questionable. Limiting access to geospatial information that is readily available from multiple sources is only likely to generate a false sense of security that has the added disadvantage of diverting attention and resources away from taking more effective homeland security measures.

A very diverse range of geospatial data and information sources exist that could be exploited by attackers trying to meet their target identification information needs. Given the ready availability of alternative data sources, restricting public access to such geospatial information sources is unlikely to be a major impediment for attackers in gaining the needed information for identifying and locating their desired U.S. targets.

The key exception to this general expectation is any type of geospatial information that reveals the location of vulnerabilities in the critical infrastructure that are not obvious or widely known, such as a particular choke point in a major power grid or telecommunications network. Compared with the ready availability of information that permits target identification and location, useful attack planning information for a particular critical infrastructure facility is much more difficult to find in publicly available sources. Given this condition of "information scarcity," any publicly available sources providing this type of detailed and timely information (e.g., internal facility equipment layout details or specifics on the security perimeter) should be more closely examined concerning their potential sensitivity for homeland security.

Filter 3: Weighing the Societal Benefits and Costs of Restricting Public Access to Geospatial Information

A final analytical filter should weigh the relative societal benefits and costs of restricting access to all or part of a particular geospatial dataset. Any decision to restrict public access needs to take into full account whether the expected homeland security benefits outweigh the likely societal costs of limiting public information access. Decisionmakers therefore have a responsibility to consider these costs, even if such costs can only be roughly gauged.

Federal geospatial information is made publicly accessible because of the many benefits it provides the public. There is a wide range of users of such federal geospatial information, including other federal agencies and state and local governments that use the information to improve public services. Government contractors and other private firms also need such information. And community groups need information to know what is happening in their community. In many cases, restricting access to the geospatial information will affect the many diverse users who need it. We highlight eight benefits of public access to geospatial information:

- **Public safety and basic transportation access needs.** People who are working, recreating, or living near a critical site need the geospatial information about the site to access or avoid the location when conducting their activities. For example, the boating, fishing, and oil and gas industry need nautical charts that show the locations of offshore oil and gas infrastructure for their work to avoid dangerous encounters or to know how to reach them for business purposes.
- **Emergency preparedness and response.** Geospatial information about critical sites is needed by emergency responders and planners to prepare for and provide services to the sites and surrounding communities in the event of a natural disaster, accident, or terrorist incident.[1] For example, local emergency responders require current and detailed geospatial information that can be shared among local agencies and with surrounding jurisdictions to ensure that appropriate preparedness activities are undertaken.
- **Improving the efficiency of government.** Publicly accessible geospatial information helps improve federal, state, and local

---

[1] The tension between addressing day-to-day public safety needs and the need to hedge against making it easier for terrorists to identify targets and undertake attackers reappears in other important questions involving emergency preparedness. For example, a similar debate is occurring over what will be the consequences of altering the use of highly visible placards required on vehicles transporting hazardous materials, which first responders need for identifying hazmat situations. See Eversole (2002, p. 12).

government efficiency in a variety of ways, including the saving of taxpayer dollars and improving data quality and public services.[2] Geospatial information is shared and made publicly accessible to reduce the duplication of data collection and maintenance by leveraging geospatial data across organizations and by using it for multiple purposes. Data are collected and maintained by one organization while being accessible to many users who otherwise would have produced their own. Publicly accessible information also improves government accountability. This trend is consistent with the growing federal government emphasis on "e-government" approaches to government-public interactions.[3]

- **Economic benefits.** Publicly accessible geospatial information is one of the key elements in the information revolution that provides many primary and secondary benefits to the U.S. economy. It is widely estimated that geographical information plays a prominent role in U.S. economic activities.[4] Hence, broad access to geospatial data and information is integral to increasing productivity, reducing private- and public-sector costs of doing business, facilitating knowledge sharing, and enhancing U.S. international competitiveness. These advantages result from the ability to widely share geospatial information through the Internet, data clearinghouses, and other means. Among private-sector users are the reseller companies that add value to federal geospatial information and sell derived products to the public.

---

[2] For example, EPA saves staff time and taxpayers dollars by making TRI data easily accessible through an interactive mapping system on the Web rather than using staff time to respond to such requests.

[3] One of the President's e-government initiatives is the Geospatial One-Stop, which will accelerate implementation of the National Spatial Data Infrastructure by providing "government agencies, data users, customers, managers, and private citizens access to geospatial information over the Internet through a One-Stop portal" ("Geospatial One-Stop," 2002, pp. 1–2).

[4] For example, one in-depth study observed that geographical information "plays a role in about one-half of the economic activities of the United States," including key sectors such as agriculture, transportation, land management, and community development (NAPA, 1998, p. 11).

The transportation area has many such resellers of U.S. Census TIGER data and USGS topographical maps. Similarly, state and local governments gain economic benefits by using publicly accessible geospatial information to, for example, attract outside businesses to locate in their areas.

- **Improving federal, state, and local government collaboration.** Making federal geospatial information accessible to state and local governments helps improve intragovernment collaboration because the different levels of government can now use the same information and save on data acquisition and maintenance costs. It can also help different levels of government develop common standards, data dictionaries, and communication protocols.

- **Improving scientific understanding.** University researchers and other scientists use federal geospatial information in their research. For example, environmental and earth scientists who study physical, chemical, and biological properties employ federal geospatial information (e.g., USGS hydrological and geological data and NASA earth science data) to improve basic scientific understanding of the earth and environment.

- **Legal and regulatory purposes.** Geospatial information is made publicly available for important legal and regulatory purposes. One of the most significant legal issues concerns community right-to-know laws, which give citizens public access to much geospatial information regarding potential critical sites in their communities. The federal Emergency Planning and Community Right to Know Act gives citizens the right to know, for example, about toxic chemicals being released into their communities to help prepare for and respond to possible chemical spills and similar emergencies.

- **Easing the reporting burden on the public.** Geospatial information is also made available to the public, often through interactive Web sites, so that citizens can more efficiently deliver information to federal agencies. For example, environmental regulations require that industries report different types of information on hazardous and toxic substances to EPA. The agency has created public Web sites (such as the Biennial

Reporting System, as discussed in Appendix C) so that companies can more easily report their information to federal agencies.

Quantifying the Benefits of Public Access to Geospatial Information

As part of this project, RAND was asked to evaluate the possible societal benefits and costs of restricting public access to geospatial information from federal agencies. A literature review on material and methodologies indicated that little research progress has been made in measuring the benefits of public access to geospatial information and much basic analytical work remains to be done. A few interesting cases exist, but analysis needed for assessing the fundamental questions raised in this project is lacking. This shortage of quantifiable information stems from a variety of reasons, including the fact that widespread sharing and publicly accessible geospatial information is a fairly recent phenomena. It is also, quite simply, difficult to quantify the basic benefits that accrue from publicly accessible geospatial information.

Many of the same difficulties arise in research attempting to quantify the benefits of GIS investments. In addition, GIS benefits literature lays out some of the initial methodological groundwork for trying to quantify the benefits of publicly accessible geospatial information.

Some important insights can be made by briefly reviewing the state of the art in making quantitative assessments of the benefits of using geospatial data, particularly in the form of GIS. Benefit and cost ratios for GIS benefits have been calculated in a number of different application areas to show the benefits and convince managers to invest in such applications. Benefit and cost ratios range as high as 10:1 or more[5] and depend on how the system and information are used.[6]

---

[5] Bernhardsen (1999, p. 23).

[6] In one international study, it was found that for more limited application areas, such as map production, the benefit-cost ratio is 1:1, and for map production and the internal use of data the benefit-cost ratio is 2:1. Applications in which there are also shared use of data, the benefit-cost ratio is 4:1 (Bernhardsen, 1999, p. 23). These numbers are based on analyzing

Benefits from GIS applications, as for publicly accessible geospatial information, include both efficiency and effectiveness benefits. *Efficiency* benefits are those that result when a GIS is used to reduce costs for a task that was previously being completed without a GIS. *Effectiveness* benefits occur when a GIS is used to perform a task that would not or could not have been done without the GIS, or improves the quality of the task being done. Efficiency benefits are easier to quantify, so many benefit and cost studies often measure only efficiency benefits. In an analysis of 62 federal government case studies of applying GIS during the early 1990s, benefit and cost ratios for efficiency benefits ranged from 1.2 to 5.6.[7] Montana has looked at both efficiency and effectiveness benefits within its state and local governments to improve the use of geospatial information. However, it has also had a difficult time quantifying effectiveness benefits.[8] Examples of benefits that are more difficult to quantify include improved decisionmaking, improved information and services provided to customers or the general public, increased public safety, and improved environmental quality or other quality-of-life enhancements.

These examples collectively illustrate how GIS benefits can be challenging to quantify, and, if they are quantified, the full benefits are often underestimated. However, organizations recognize such benefits even if they are not captured by formal means. For example, Kerr County, Texas, has used GIS to improve tax assessments, such as finding properties that were not on the tax rolls. In discussing the benefits of GIS, the Kerr County Chief Appraiser mentions the story of a rancher who tried to dispute his tax appraisal. The rancher claimed his property was not worth that much, since he did not have water on it. Using the GIS system, he displayed the rancher's property in an aerial photomap that showed it was right next to the Guadalupe River. The rancher dropped his complaint, which he may

---

50–60 organizations throughout the United States, Canada, Italy, Norway, Sweden, Denmark, Finland, and Iceland.

[7] Gillespie (1997). See also Gillespie (1994a; 1994b).

[8] McInnis and Blundell (1998).

have taken to the Appraisal Review Board without the GIS data (Texas Association of Counties, 1999a). The same types of benefits, and difficulties, in quantifying them occur with publicly accessible geospatial information.

Despite these shortfalls in being able to quantify the societal benefits associated with public access to geospatial information sources, it is nonetheless important for decisionmakers to at least recognize the likelihood that publicly accessible geospatial sources from federal agencies and others are being used for diverse purposes and may have substantial public benefits. Thus, decisions on restricting public access should seek to identify the range of potential information users and at least qualitatively assess the opportunity costs for these users if their access to particular pieces of geospatial information is curtailed in some way.

Illustrating the Framework

How would decisionmakers apply this framework? The process would vary somewhat depending on the responsibilities of particular federal decisionmakers. Decisionmakers focused on assessing the homeland security implications of a particular type or piece of publicly accessible geospatial information would use the framework to identify how public access to the geospatial information could affect the ability of adversaries, including terrorist groups, to undertake attacks on various types of U.S. critical infrastructure facilities or key assets. In comparison, other decisionmakers would be focused on the operational security, including information protection needs, of particular critical sites. These decisionmakers could range from individuals who are site managers for a particular critical site (e.g., dam, chemical plant), a general type of critical infrastructure (e.g., pipelines, nuclear power plants), or even an information protection program for all critical U.S. sites. Despite differing responsibilities, each type of decisionmaker can use this framework to gain relevant insights in identifying potentially sensitive geospatial information.[9]

For any type of decisionmaker interested in assessing the homeland security implications of publicly available geospatial information, the filtering questions should be applied sequentially. Table 4.3 provides a set of illustrative questions to provide a sense of the types

Table 4.3
Illustrative Use of the Filters

Filter	Key Questions for Decisionmakers
1. Usefulness	• Is the publicly accessible geospatial information useful for target selection purposes?
	—Does the information provide details that are not common knowledge, which identify particular critical sites?
	—Does the information provide specific and accurate geolocation coordinates?
	—Does the information provide insights on choke points within a critical infrastructure sector?
	—Is the information relatively current, or is it dated (and does that matter)?
	• Is the geospatial information useful for attack planning purposes?
	—Does the information identify key internal features?
	—Does the information provide details on facility layout and vulnerabilities?
	—Does the information provide insights into operational practices at critical sites?
	—Is the information relatively current, or is it dated (and does that matter)?
2. Uniqueness	• Is the information readily available from other geospatial information sources?
	—Web sites, including archived Internet sites?
	—Hard-copy maps?

_____

[9] This analysis assumes that risk communication mechanisms allowing information sharing will evolve over time, presumably with the Department of Homeland Security's (DHS's) leadership and encouragement, to help ensure that decisionmakers responsible for the protection of U.S. critical sites against attack will receive information relevant to their efforts, including assessments on potentially sensitive geospatial data and information that is publicly accessible.

Table 4.3—Continued

Filter	Key Questions for Decisionmakers
Uniqueness (cont.)	—Textual documents? —GIS databases? • Is the information available from nongeospatial information sources? —Is direct access or direct observation by potential attackers feasible? —Can attackers' information needs be met using general engineering and technical expertise?
3. Societal Benefits and Costs	• What are the expected security benefits of restricting public access to this geospatial information? —Will restricting public access to specific geospatial information significantly increase the difficulty of potential attackers to undertake effective attacks against U.S. critical sites? —What is the estimated possible damage (e.g., casualties, infrastructure disruption, estimated financial costs) that could be avoided or minimized if public access to certain geospatial information is restricted? • What are the expected societal costs of restricting public access to this geospatial information? —Do people who live, work, or recreate near particular locations need this information for physically accessing (or avoiding) particular locations? —Does the information need to be publicly accessible for public safety purposes (e.g., pipeline locations, hazardous chemical facilities)? —Is the information publicly available for legal reasons (e.g., community right-to-know laws)? —Who are the main users of the information (e.g., businesses, state or local governments, universities, NGOs, the general public)? How much do they depend on publicly accessible information? —Do domestic users have alternative sources of comparable information at similar costs? —What are the estimated costs to primary users if public access to this information is restricted? • What are the expected costs to the information supplier for imposing restrictive measures on information access?

of detailed questions that would be relevant to using each of the three filters. Although some questions are not likely to yield precise or easily quantifiable answers, they are still useful to consider in assessing the homeland security implications of publicly available geospatial information.

Filter 1: Assessing Usefulness. In applying the first filter concerning the possible usefulness of the publicly accessible information for potential attackers, the decisionmaker initially needs to determine which critical sites the database contains information about. The next question concerns what type of information the database provides about the critical site. As Table 4.3 highlights, the decisionmaker is interested in determining whether a particular piece of publicly available geospatial information can pose a security problem by assisting potential attackers with information they need for either target selection/location or specific attack planning. A particularly important question in this filter is whether there is a temporal dimension to the attacker's information needs. In other words, does it matter whether the information is new or old? Will the attacker need relatively current information to have confidence in undertaking a successful attack, or can geospatial information that is years old be sufficient for attack planning purposes? In identifying information that is potentially useful for target selection and location purposes, it is important to focus on detailed information rather than information that is common knowledge.

Filter 2: Assessing Uniqueness. Assuming that a particular piece of geospatial information is assessed to be useful for either the target selection/location or the attack planning needs of a potential attacker, it would then be subject to the second filter. The decisionmaker uses this filter to examine whether potential attackers can satisfy their critical mission information needs through alternative sources or whether the geospatial information in question is relatively unique. Alternative information sources could come from nonfederal geospatial sources (e.g., private sector; state or local government) that are publicly available. In addition, the decisionmaker will want to give special consideration to whether the attacker could obtain comparable (or better-quality) information by taking advantage of nongeospatial sources. These sources could include direct access to, or observation of, a potential target. A key consideration is whether potential attackers would run unacceptable risks of being detected and caught while exploiting opportunities for direct reconnaissance of a potential target. Furthermore, how much useful attack information the attacker can gain from drawing on basic engineering and technical expertise also needs to be considered, since it could be readily available on various U.S. critical sites and enable the attacker to avoid the risks of being detected.

Filter 3: Societal Benefits and Costs. Finally, geospatial information that is both useful to potential attackers and not readily available from alternative sources should be considered potentially sensitive from a homeland security perspective. This information should be subjected to the third filter that helps decisionmakers weigh the likely societal benefits and costs of restricting public access to the information. The best cases for restricting public access will be those in which a reasonable expectation exists for improving homeland security. If decisionmakers can determine that the potential societal costs of imposing restrictions on information access are relatively limited, the expected benefits of restricting public access become even greater. This assessment should consider the true security benefits and societal costs to users and providers of the information. However, making an assessment of societal costs is likely to be complicated by the diverse range of public- and private-sector users of a particular type of geospatial information, as well as the likelihood that they will have varying degrees of access to alternative information sources if restrictions are imposed. Nonetheless, even if specific quantifiable assessments of societal benefits and costs are not possible, decisionmakers should at least make explicit qualitative judgments on the expected homeland security benefits of restricting public access to all or part of a geospatial information dataset, as well as offer their best estimate of the potential societal costs. Even rough assessments could be helpful in choosing among a range of options for restricting public access to all or part of federal geospatial information datasets.

Although this analytical filter can assist U.S. decisionmakers in better understanding the key considerations at stake, making good decisions on striking the correct balance among competing considerations is likely to be challenging. Thus, it will be important to ensure that basic decisions on restricting or reinstituting public access to geospatial information are considered that permit both the potential security benefits and possible societal costs to be impartially weighed. This task is complicated by the possibility that some stakeholders are likely to find that highlighting, or even exaggerating, the likely homeland security benefits or societal costs is the best strategy for protecting their interests. Thus, key decisions on restricting public access on geospatial information will be best made in a process that allows senior U.S. decisionmakers to make impartial judgments on the relative merits of these complex choices in light of the competing interests of stakeholders on both sides of the issues.

Options and Precedents for Permitting Conditional Public Access

Identifying sensitive information does not necessarily preclude some form of conditional public access. It is worth remembering that conditional public access to sensitive information is not a new problem for the United States.[10] Government agencies have long had legal requirements and administrative practices for limiting public access to unclassified information for a variety of reasons, including the need to protect privacy and proprietary information. At least two types of options exist for making information publicly accessible by reducing its potential sensitivity or limiting access to users with legitimate needs for the information: dataset structure and user access conditions.

Data Structure. Government agencies often collect data that involve sensitive information if released in a raw form or a specific level of detail. For example, U.S. Census datasets are made publicly available at a higher level of aggregation to avoid releasing potentially sensitive information that could affect the privacy of individuals and

---

[10] For an example of how alternative institution mechanisms can be developed for making potentially sensitive environmental data derived from U.S. intelligence systems available in unclassified forms for civilian and academic users, see Pace, O'Connell, and Lachman (1997, pp. 39–54).

families. Some important precedents exist as well for limiting public access to unclassified information, including some well-known cases of withholding certain detailed geospatial datasets from the public that are concerned with protecting endangered species and archeological sites. Similarly, known geospatial information that would, for example, help the public to identify the locations of unfamiliar caves is not placed on maps for public safety and preservation purposes. The option exists in cases in which geospatial datasets have been identified with homeland security implications to explore ways of eliminating or greatly diminishing the usefulness of the information for potential attackers by eliminating particular data attributes. Other options are generalizing certain types of data or reducing the timeliness of certain types of data in ways that could retain the general utility for legitimate domestic users of the geospatial information.

User Access Conditions. Another option for dealing with potentially sensitive information is placing access conditions to increase the chances that only legitimate users will have access to potentially sensitive information. Precedents have been set in permitting individual access to important geospatial information in government reading rooms. For example, although EPA off-site consequence analysis (i.e., for the so-called worst-case scenario) for U.S. facilities that maintain potentially hazardous chemicals on-site is accessible at EPA reading rooms, the same information is not available online for easy and anonymous access.[11] Similarly, access to specific federal agency information concerning archeological sites can be obtained if the user provides adequate identification and justification for needing such information, as well as agreement to nondisclosure restrictions.

Thus, decisionmakers have various options for dealing with sensitive geospatial information. Restricting access is less likely to require a complete denial of public access and is more likely to involve some limited restrictions on the data content—or the institution of some

---

[11] For example, see the discussion in U.S. Congress (2001).

identification and authentication procedures for some types of public users.

Considerations in Restricting Public Access to Sensitive Data

In addition to the filters that our framework sets up, decisionmakers must also consider further factors relating to how precisely they might carry out any restriction. A variety of options, as well as precedents, exist for restricting public access to federal geospatial information sources. In addition, since our analysis showed that geospatial information is spread across a diverse range of federal and nonfederal sources, controlling any particular type or piece of data is difficult if the objective is enhancing security, especially because potential attackers could exploit the diverse sources.

Before restricting access to a geospatial dataset, a federal agency or other organization needs to assess the full impact of restricting public access to geospatial data and information sources. This includes determining the true security demands and assessing the many different benefits, just discussed, that would be lost. An important part of this process is evaluating the current and potential future users of the information. An assessment also needs to be made to quantify what effect the restriction will have on the economy, including long-term and secondary impacts. The likely legal, political, and public fallout also must be considered. Recognition that only certain attributes of a dataset may need to be restricted should also be an important consideration in this assessment process. Finally, consideration of the economic cost associated with restricting a dataset or parts of a dataset, and ensuring that it is continually protected, needs to be included in the evaluation process.

Federal, State, and Local Government Concerns About Restricting Federal Data Access

In our discussions with federal, state, and local government security and geospatial data experts, important issues, concerns, and insights about the possibility of restricting data access to federal geospatial information were raised.

We found that, for selected sensitive data, federal agencies are thinking of restricting or limiting selected future data features or attributes that are considered to have the most sensitive homeland security implications. However, because of the users who need such information, federal agencies also are considering how to provide such information to key users and for priority uses, such as instituting password access through the Web for emergency planners and responders. In many cases, the officials noted that it would be costly and physically difficult to restrict access to a geospatial dataset or selected attributes within that dataset. First, since data are already distributed in many places and since other federal agencies, federal regional offices, value-added resellers, NGOs, and states also distribute data, it would be difficult to recall existing data. TRI and USGS DOQs and topographical maps are both good examples of geospatial datasets that are widely distributed and difficult to contain. Second, as noted above, the actual cost of restricting access—namely, the cost of developing, implementing, and enforcing procedures to limit access to the information—could be high. Third, restricting access to geospatial information would often create additional risks and costs for many diverse users who need the information for important reasons, such as for public safety, as discussed above.

Public confidence was a concern that federal, state, and local agencies raised in considering public access to geospatial information. Some individuals want to restrict access to previously publicly accessible or newly developed geospatial information to avoid the perception that the information is easily accessible to attackers—even if the public release of the information poses no measurable security risk to the critical site.

In our discussions, we also found that there tends to be two diverse orientations for viewing geospatial information by individuals within most federal and state organizations. If there are no clear security concerns, most geospatial data experts and providers want the data to be in the public domain, both for the many users and the numerous benefits the data provide. Conversely, many security managers want to restrict information access as much as possible, even if restricting access does not enhance security, because of the aforementioned public confidence concerns.

This report provides a general conceptual framework for thinking about the factors that should be of concern when determining whether access to geospatial information should be restricted in the hopes of addressing homeland security concerns. The proposed framework is just a start on a larger analytical process because it only introduces the key questions to be addressed and highlights important factors for consideration by decisionmakers. However, it does not in itself provide sufficient guidance for a consistent and broad application of the principles presented in this paper to the wide variety of U.S. critical sites and the need to protect against diverse types of threats. The following section introduces the idea of a more formal model for implementing elements of the framework and discusses some of the key elements that would be desirable in a more formal model to identifying and managing sensitive geospatial information.

Long-Term Need for a More Comprehensive Model

The analytical framework presented in this study offers an explicit and useful tool for decisionmakers at the early stage of identifying the potentially sensitive types of publicly available geospatial information (i.e., information that is both useful to an attacker and has relatively few alternatives). Any information protection approach designed for geospatial information should be based on a relatively rigorous operation of establishing the desired impacts at different levels of protection and the actual steps needed to protect the data. While the framework presented in this report serves as a useful interim step, a more formal and comprehensive model is desirable for the longer term.

One of the difficulties in developing a viable protection strategy is that, in the decentralized U.S. system, there is a need to have all the entities (private, local, state, and federal) acting in harmony. Typical command-and-control models for security have limited applicability for the government, since there are the twin problems of establishing a meaningful level of compliance in a huge population and of transmitting useful guidance on what to do under a wide variety of possible circumstances.[12] The latter point is critical because one of the deficiencies in most command-and-control approaches is their inability to apply to the local situation in a manner that would both enhance homeland security and impose the smallest negative impact from implementing the protection mechanisms.

A key step, from our standpoint, is the development of a set of well-defined protection levels that can be associated with a formal threat and protection matrix. This matrix would need to take a comprehensive approach to assessing possible attackers and resources at their disposal to gather information, the availability of the information, and the sensitivity of the data in terms of possible consequence of the compromise of confidentiality, loss of data integrity, or loss of availability. The matrix would also help by (1) establishing a common definition of the types of attacks the security system would need to be tested against, (2) assisting designers in understanding the required activities during design and fielding to establish that level of protection, and (3) functioning as a mechanism for evaluating the end products.

A useful feature of this approach is that it separates the establishment of protection levels from the types of installations that might need to be protected. One of the most contentious issues is determining the appropriate level for an installation. The issue is complicated because, above and beyond the protection decision for the geo-

---

[12] In the United States, command-and-control models for security have little precedent outside a narrow range of activities in which federal issues are at stake. These issues have included national security, and those such as nuclear safety that have been born as federal issues. Homeland defense would seem to be one of the issues that would likewise trigger intervention. Unfortunately, in this model, effective federal action would likely need to be so pervasive (identifying which kinds of information, protection strategies, needs for information system, and physical security of the data) that it would be quite cumbersome in operation.

spatial information, a host of related decisions emerge related to other aspects of facility and information protection.

A seldom-appreciated issue outside the security community is that information protection levels necessarily imply associated levels of physical, communications, procedural, and personnel security that would seriously affect the cost and attractiveness of security measures. This linkage means that, in practice, the highest level of security would be associated with facilities and installations that really need *and* can afford the costs of the security system.

Any information protection strategy implicitly has a set of assumptions as to *from whom* the data is being protected. The most stringent level of protection might be targeted at denying critical bits of information from nation-state intelligence services with extraordinary capabilities of gathering information. The small amount of geospatially associated information might represent information from denied facilities critical for operational functions. Lower levels of protection would defend against progressively lesser threats. The basic information floor for an adversary might be marked by what is readily discernable with expert observation of external features using common commercial products or obtainable from publicly available sources.

Having access to the potential insights that can be generated by the framework for analysis for assessing the homeland security implications of geospatial information sources, as presented earlier, would be very useful in developing a more comprehensive information protection model. Decisionmakers responsible for the information protection of particular U.S. facilities and installations, or even entire critical infrastructure sectors, need timely insights on what types of publicly available geospatial information could have important homeland security implications. Although multiple mechanisms will probably evolve over time for conveying such insights, DHS is likely to play a leading role in ensuring that any assessment of the potential sensitivity of geospatial data and information sources is conveyed to relevant critical infrastructure sectors and other types of key national assets through all appropriate public- and private-sector channels, including industry-sponsored Information Sharing and Analysis Centers. Similarly, U.S. Northern Command (NORTHCOM) is likely to ensure that those responsible for operational security at DoD installations are aware of any assessments concerning publicly available geospatial information that could affect the protection of their facilities and activities.

Constructing the initial matrix will be challenging, but it is perhaps the most important step in ensuring that the overall system for information protection will be properly set up. The following are key issues that will need to be addressed in formulating and implementing a more comprehensive and formal approach to information protection.

- **Threat Model.** The development of standardized threat models is vital, since it will drive the design of the detailed protection strategies. Choices need to be made as to whether the degree of the threat will be regarded purely as an outsider threat or whether insiders are to be considered in the threat space. Decisions as to the probable sophistication of possible attackers also will have to be made to get a handle on possible modalities of attack.

- **Assurance.** Tough decisions will have to be made as to the level of assurance desired for the protection level. Which levels constitute high-assurance protection? Which are essentially schemes to allow security to be tipped off to actions and slow attackers? Which are markers to warn off the casual snooper? Simply saying the information needs to be protected neglects these issues and the very real costs involved in attempting simply to implement a security schema.

- **Protection Levels.** The next step in instituting an effective security system is to begin associating specific set actions in the physical, information protection, and personnel realms that would be associated with the desired total level of protection. The goal here would be to avoid associating an inappropriate protection measure with an incorrect threat and protection level. For instance, in the context of computer network security, if the protection level is relatively low, imposing requirements for protecting against adversary use of unintended emissions for information systems would be inappropriate; however, protecting against a site operating an unsecured wireless network access point might be very appropriate.

- **Certification Process.** Once a system has been designed, it is important to consider how to assess whether or not protection levels have been achieved. Will it be a process-oriented standard in which going through the right procedures will yield a certification? Will it be certified by an assessment group? A process-oriented approach probably would not be adequate on its own, since it is quite possible to build an insecure system from secure elements. An auditing approach that allows some level of site monitoring would be appropriate to determine how well the standard is being followed. The whole issue of certification is complex and would require further analysis as to which approach would be best.

- **Facility Selection.** Finally, the big issue of deciding which groups of facilities should be included in the security model also needs consideration. The issue is clearly contentious, and there will be serious matters in regard to how the decision should be made and what the factors are that should determine the association of facilities with different security levels. Should it be based on damage to U.S. national security issues, loss of life, economic factors, or other aspects? If it is a mix, as it probably will be, what is the correct weighting? Outside a few cases, there may be no consensus as to how the rules should be applied. However, the development of the guidelines will tend to make it easier for groups to do the right thing, and potentially allow approaches based on market forces, such as through insurance and liability, to be used to motivate desirable action.

The end result of this comprehensive process is the development of a set of standards for protection levels that could be used and implemented in a decentralized manner. Outside of a handful of sectors, enforcement might be limited to government regulations that mandate a minimal protection level. In general, these standards would permit site managers to pick and choose what level is appropriate for their facility or installation and allow those with limited homeland security and national security experience to make better choices regarding the balance of protection measures. Although there is no expectation that recommended comprehensive model will yield precise answers, it offers a more formal process for integrating relevant expertise and encouraging greater consistency among the information protection decisions that must be made by U.S. federal and nonfederal decisionmakers regarding diverse U.S. critical sites.

Summary

U.S. decisionmakers need an analytical framework that helps them to identify and assess potentially sensitive geospatial information that is publicly accessible from federal agencies. In addition, the framework should help to at least structure the relevant questions as to whether restricting public access to certain geospatial information is likely to improve U.S. homeland security without imposing unacceptable societal costs in other key areas.

The framework for analysis presented in this report is a useful first step that can provide an explicit and consistent process for weighing salient considerations related to assessing the homeland security sensitivity of publicly available geospatial information. Over the longer term, a more formal and comprehensive model for information protection involving U.S. critical sites will be required and should address the key considerations highlighted in this chapter. In the meantime, however, the analytical framework outlined in this chapter serves as a useful start. It identifies key factors that federal agency decisionmakers should explicitly consider in determining whether and how to restrict public access to geospatial data and information available from their organizations for the purpose of improving homeland security. In addition, the framework is generally applicable to all other decisionmakers in the public and private sectors who must make practical decisions on geospatial information protection issues for homeland security purposes.

CHAPTER FIVE

Key Findings and Recommendations

An integral element of homeland security is minimizing the opportunities for adversaries to acquire essential information for undertaking attacks on critical U.S. sites. Publicly available geospatial data and information are a potentially valuable type of information that attackers could exploit to help identify critical U.S. facilities and then carry out their attack plans. Thus, denying adversaries access to any type of "sensitive" geospatial information is important to enhancing U.S. homeland security. Placing access restrictions on this kind of data and information, however, should be based on a reasonable expectation of improving U.S. homeland security given that such restrictions are likely to involve societal costs of various types.

Key Findings

This study presents several key findings on the potential homeland security implications of geospatial data and information sources, particularly those made publicly accessible by U.S. federal agencies. First, our analyses of the attacker *demand* for and the existing *supply* of geospatial data yielded several specific findings.

"Demand" Analysis Findings
Our analysis of potential attackers' information needs for undertaking attacks on critical U.S. sites produced the following findings:

Attackers have substantial flexibility in fulfilling their information needs for attacking U.S. homeland locations. In principle, this flexibility includes a broad range of choices about why, where, and how attacks will be made against U.S. homeland locations by possible attackers, such as terrorist groups or hostile governments. This flexibility has important implications for the types of information that attackers need and can acquire for target selection and identification and for attack planning purposes. Our demand assessment of attackers' information requirements suggests that, given the degree of flexibility, publicly accessible geospatial information is probably not an attacker's first choice for fulfilling information needs. Although such information has the potential to be somewhat useful in selecting a target and determining its location, attackers are more likely to desire more reliable information obtainable via other means, such as direct access or observation of possible U.S. homeland targets. In addition, many types of attacks, such as those carried out by ground parties, are likely to require detailed information for attack planning purposes, although they would largely depend on the target type and mode of attack. This type of information, which mostly comes from such nongeospatial sources as engineering textbooks or human expertise on the operations of a particular type of industrial complex, is essential for attackers to have high confidence in an attack plan.

As opportunistic attackers, terrorists usually possess the advantage of having access to diverse sources for meeting their mission-critical information needs, as well as the freedom to adjust the attack to meet the amount of information available. An important distinction exists between what is critical information for the attacker (i.e., information in which the attacker could not perform the attack without), what is useful but not necessary to undertake the attack, and what is nonessential information. Lacking critical information on a target could, in theory, discourage an attacker from proceeding with a given attack. In practice, however, an opportunistic attacker can exploit diverse information sources (ranging from direct observation to publicly available geospatial information) to meet critical information needs, while the defender faces the challenge of denying the attacker access to all relevant sources of information. The attacker can also change the mode of attack to better match the amount and type of information available. For example, if information is unavailable to support a direct assault on a target, standoff attacks on a different part of the complex or attacks outside the most heavily defended area producing the same or similar effect could be substituted. Similarly, if detailed plans are unavailable on a target to facilitate use of precisely placed munitions, weapons with a larger area of impact or different phenomenology might be used to produce the desired effect.

"Supply" Analysis Findings

The supply analysis of publicly accessible geospatial data and information from federal agencies and other potential sources produced the following findings:

Our federal geospatial information survey found that publicly available geospatial information is spread across a wide range of federal government agencies and offices. Many different agencies are major distributors of publicly available geospatial information. We identified 465 programs, offices, or major initiatives at 30 different federal agencies and departments that make various types of geospatial information publicly accessible.

Our analysis found that very few of the publicly accessible federal geospatial sources appear useful to meeting a potential attacker's information needs. We examined a sample of 629 federal geospatial information datasets that appeared to contain data or information related to various types of U.S. critical sites. Based on a closer examination, we concluded that fewer than 6 percent of these federal geospatial datasets appeared useful for providing information that could help an attacker with selecting a target or planning an attack against a site. Furthermore, we found no publicly available federal geospatial datasets that we considered critical to meeting attacker needs (i.e., those that the attacker could not perform the attack without).

Our analysis also suggests that most publicly accessible federal geospatial information is unlikely to provide significant (i.e., both useful and unique) information for satisfying attackers' information needs. Along with assessing whether the federal datasets contained potentially useful information for attackers, we also assessed whether the federal sources were relatively unique (i.e., that they provide geospatial information not readily available from alternative sources). We concluded that fewer than 1 percent of the 629 federal datasets examined appeared to be both potentially useful and unique. Furthermore, since 9/11, these information sources are no longer being made public by federal agencies. However, we cannot conclude that *publicly accessible* geospatial information from federal agencies provides no special benefit to the attacker. Neither can we conclude that it would benefit the attacker. Our sample does suggest, however, that the publicly available federal geospatial information of potential homeland security concern, if it exists, is not distributed widely and may be scarce.

In many cases, diverse alternative geospatial and nongeospatial information sources exist for meeting the information needs of potential attackers. We identified and sampled more than 300 publicly available nonfederal geospatial information alternative sources that provide geospatial information on U.S. critical sites. Our sampling of nonfederal geospatial data sources suggests that the same, similar, or more useful geospatial information on U.S. critical sites is available from a diverse set of nonfederal sources, which include industry and commercial businesses, academic institutions, NGOs, state and local governments, international suppliers, and even private citizens who publish their own relevant materials on the Internet. In addition, relevant information is often available from the direct access or direct observation that is possible for most U.S. homeland locations.

Broader Implications

In addition to the specific findings, our analysis produced several broader implications. These observations concern the general nature of geospatial information sources, the usefulness of geospatial information for potential attackers against U.S. homeland locations, and the role that the federal government could play in providing guidance to agencies about whether and how to restrict such information.

The ability of potential attackers to exploit publicly available geospatial information significantly varies with the type of information needed. With some important exceptions, the information needed for identifying and locating potential targets is widely accessible. In comparison, detailed and up-to-date information required for attack planning against a particular target is much less readily available from publicly available sources. A diverse range of geospatial data and information sources exists that could be exploited by attackers trying to meet their target identification information needs. Given the ready availability of alternative data sources, restricting public access to such geospatial information is unlikely to be a major impediment for attackers in gaining the needed information for identifying and locating their desired U.S. targets. The key exception to this general expectation is any type of geospatial information that reveals the location of vulnerabilities in the critical infrastructure that are not obvious or widely known, such as a particular choke point in a major power grid or telecommunications network. Compared with the ready availability of information that permits target identification and location, useful attack planning information for a particular critical infrastructure facility is much more difficult to find in publicly available sources. Given this condition of "information scarcity," any publicly available sources providing this type of detailed and timely information (e.g., internal facility equipment layout details, specifics on the security perimeter and procedures) should be examined more closely concerning their potential sensitivity for homeland security.

Our results do not rule out the possibility that federal publicly available geospatial information could be exploited by potential attackers, including the possibility that discrete pieces of publicly accessible geospatial information could be aggregated by the attacker with the aim of achieving greater targeting value than is apparent when the information is viewed separately. However, these pieces of information should be identified in the context of how they might be specifically used by potential attackers. In addition, because widely available nonfederal sources often exist with similar geospatial information, alternative sources need to be assessed. Therefore, an analytical process is needed to evaluate individual geospatial datasets concerning their potential risks for protecting U.S. critical sites and whether restrictions to public access will enhance homeland security.

Decisions about whether and how to restrict geospatial information would benefit from applying an analytic framework to help assess the sensitivity of a piece of geospatial information being publicly available and the security benefits and societal costs of restricting public access. The analytical approach presented in this study integrates three distinct filters—*usefulness, uniqueness,* and *societal benefits and costs*—as a first-step framework for decisionmakers to help evaluate whether a geospatial dataset is conceivably sensitive, and whether public access should be curtailed in some way. An explicit framework for analysis offers decisionmakers several benefits including a way of making more structured and uniform decisions on whether and how to restrict public access to geospatial information, as well as a better way of explaining the basis for such decisions to others.

Assessing the societal benefits and costs of restricting public access to geospatial information is not straightforward. Along with assessing the expected security benefits of restricting public access to certain types of geospatial information, this analytical framework seeks to weigh the societal costs of limiting public access. Most publicly available geospatial information addresses particular public and private needs for such information, including public safety, health, economic development, and other purposes. However, gauging the costs of restricting public access is complicated by limitations in existing methodologies for quantifying the specific benefits and costs of public access to geospatial information. Key decisions on restricting public access on geospatial information will be best made in a process that allows senior U.S. decisionmakers to make impartial judgments on the relative merits of these complex choices in light of the competing interests of stakeholders.

The federal government has a unique role in providing geospatial guidance to federal agencies, as well as insights on information sensitivity for nonfederal organizations. We conclude that U.S.

civilian and military agencies have a growing need for well-founded and consistent guidelines for identifying geospatial data and information that could have homeland security implications. In addition, nonfederal organizations also have a need for similar guidance in making decisions on information protection policies involving geospatial data and information.

General Recommendations

The main recommendation of this report is that the federal government play a proactive role in bringing greater coherence and consistency to the question of assessing the homeland security implications of publicly available geospatial information. A strong need exists among the wide range of U.S. federal agencies for practical guidance to assist decisionmakers in framing the often difficult choices on whether to place new restrictions on public access to parts of their geospatial data and information or to modify restrictions imposed after the September 11 attacks. Civilian federal agencies that produce and distribute substantial geospatial information to the public have a practical need for such guidelines. However, even DoD organizations, particularly installation managers in the United States, also need timely insights on how best to strike a balance between safeguarding potentially sensitive geospatial information on their facilities for force-protection reasons and allowing access because of the public benefits from information sharing. At the same time, installation decisionmakers need to know what type of geospatial information is safe to share with the public and private sectors to achieve efficiencies in facility management and for other purposes.

The federal government can increase the awareness of the public and private sectors concerning the potential sensitivity of geospatial information. We recommend that the federal government develop mechanisms for sharing risks assessments on the potential sensitivity of certain types of information, including geospatial information, to address near-term demands for guidance. State and local officials need to be aware of what types of geospatial information could have homeland security implications. Furthermore, given that a majority of the nation's critical infrastructure is managed by the private sector, these mechanisms need to be adapted for information sharing with senior managers at a wide range of private-sector organizations, particularly those critical infrastructure enterprises.

An analytical process should be used by federal agencies and other organizations to assess the potential homeland security sensitivity of specific pieces of geospatial information that is publicly available and whether restricting access would enhance security. The analytical framework presented earlier is a useful first step, which is immediately available, for helping federal decisionmakers to make sound and consistent decisions on whether and how to restrict public access to geospatial information. We also believe that this framework can be useful for any decisionmaker faced with determining whether and how to make specific geospatial information publicly accessible.

For the longer term, the federal government should develop a more comprehensive model for addressing the security of geospatial information. A more formal and comprehensive model should be developed to provide a means of associating desired protection levels relative to the type of threats, associated protection profiles to defeat those threats, and a structured set of evaluation criteria. Facilities and installations could be, in turn, associated with those protection levels based on the particular needs of individual facilities and installations. Such a comprehensive model would also provide public- and private-sector decisionmakers with a consistent level of protection for a wide variety of different types of facilities. It would also focus discussion away from how the data is to be protected and onto the more difficult question of what level of protection is appropriate for a given facility or installation.

Agency-Specific Recommendations

NGA and USGS should make their expertise available to support federal government policy development for identifying geospatial information with implications for homeland security. DHS, in collaboration with OMB, will likely be the lead policymaking agency in formulating policy guidelines for U.S. federal agencies for dealing with the homeland security implications of publicly available geospatial information. Similarly, NORTHCOM, which is the lead homeland defense command operation, is likely to play a major role in providing guidance to a wide range of military decisionmakers concerned with force protection at U.S. installations. These agencies should draw on the expertise on geospatial information that is already available among U.S. federal agencies.

As primary government agencies that produce and distribute geospatial data and information, NGA and USGS, should anticipate playing a substantial role in applying their special expertise to help other organizations in identifying sensitive geospatial information. Both organizations possess unique capabilities and expertise relevant to helping develop the U.S. federal government principles or guidelines for identifying sensitive geospatial information.

NGA should take advantage of its special expertise in geospatial intelligence to give other organizations a better sense of how various types of geospatial data and information can be exploited by potential adversaries to attack U.S. critical infrastructure facilities and other key locations, including military installations. NGA should leverage its expertise in the following areas:

- processing of geospatial information (e.g., tools and techniques)
- experience in supporting the geospatial information needs for military targeting
- data-integration expertise
- expertise in foreign geospatial information policies and practices.

In this context, DoD organizations, including NORTHCOM, should take advantage of NGA's expertise in evaluating the potential sensitivity of geospatial data and information for homeland security, including the need to enhance force protection at U.S. military installations.

Similarly, USGS has complementary expertise to offer in supporting the development of U.S. federal guidelines on identifying potentially sensitive geospatial information. USGS has extensive knowledge of science-based applications and a strong sense of the breadth of domestic and international sources of publicly available geospatial information, which is a key factor in assessing the relative uniqueness of this type of information source. In addition, USGS probably possesses a greater appreciation than most other federal organizations of the range of public and private stakeholders that are likely to be affected by any changes in public access to geospatial data and information.

One of the legacies of the September 11 attacks is viewing familiar public policy issues in a new light. U.S. federal agencies have long been a leading source of making information, including geospatial data and information, available to the public and private sectors. Along with the traditional reasons for placing certain restrictions on access to such information, homeland security adds a salient concern over how best to strike the balance between making geospatial information available for myriad public purposes while not releasing any information that could diminish U.S. homeland security. Based on an in-depth examination of key aspects of this issue, this report offers insights and an analytical framework for decisionmakers responsible for making the difficult decisions on ways to achieve this balance in dealing with potentially sensitive geospatial information.

Federal Agencies Examined

To identify publicly available federal geospatial information sources, we conducted a structured survey of all major federal executive and independent agencies as well as the ones most likely to contain geospatial information about U.S. critical sites.

This appendix lists the 69 federal agencies that we searched. The Department of Homeland Security (DHS) was not included because it did not exist in spring and summer 2002 when the survey was conducted; however, our survey did include agencies (e.g., the Federal Emergency Management Agency [FEMA]) and other offices that are now part of DHS.

Federal Departments

Department of Agriculture

Department of Commerce

Department of Defense

Department of Energy

Department of Health and Human Services

Department of Housing and Urban Development

Department of Justice

Department of Labor

Department of State

Department of the Interior

Department of the Treasury

Department of Transportation

Department of Veterans Affairs

Other Federal Agencies

Architect of the Capitol

Central Intelligence Agency

Commodity Futures Trading Commission

Consumer Product Safety Commission

Defense Nuclear Facilities Safety Board

Environmental Protection Agency

Equal Employment Opportunity Commission

Export-Import Bank of the United States

Farm Credit Administration

Federal Communications Commission

Federal Consumer Information Center

Federal Deposit Insurance Corporation

Federal Election Commission

Federal Emergency Management Agency

Federal Housing Finance Board

Federal Maritime Commission

Federal Mediation and Conciliation Service

Federal Mine Safety and Health Review Commission

Federal Reserve System

Federal Trade Commission

General Services Administration

International Joint Commission, Canada and the United States

Library of Congress

National Aeronautics and Space Administration

National Archives and Records Administration

National Capital Planning Commission

National Credit Union Administration

National Endowment for the Arts

National Endowment for the Humanities

National Labor Relations Board

National Mediation Board

National Railroad Passenger Corporation (Amtrak)

National Science Foundation

National Transportation Safety Board

Nuclear Regulatory Commission

Nuclear Waste Technical Review Board

Occupational Safety and Health Administration

Office of Federal Housing Enterprise Oversight

Office of Personnel Management

Overseas Private Investment Corporation

Pension Benefit Guaranty Corporation

Postal Rate Commission

Railroad Retirement Board

Securities and Exchange Commission

Selective Service System

Small Business Administration

Social Security Administration

Tennessee Valley Authority

Thrift Savings Plan

Trade and Development Agency

United States Agency for International Development

United States Arms Control and Disarmament Agency

United States District Courts

United States International Trade Commission

United States Postal Service

United States Trade and Development Agency

Federal Geospatial Data Sources Identified

This appendix contains the 465 programs, offices, or major initiatives identified at 30 different federal agencies—namely the federal publicly accessible geospatial sources that we identified. These sources, and their corresponding Web sites, were found during the data collection phase of our research from spring 2002 through summer 2002. These Web sites were revisited during our analysis process that continued through spring 2003. However, since that time, some of these agency programs, offices, and initiatives and their corresponding Web sites may have changed or gone away. In addition, there may be new programs, offices, or initiatives, or ones not identified in our extensive survey, that also make geospatial information publicly available.

In most cases, this table lists agencies and major suborganizations (such as subagencies) along with the Web site of interest for the major program, office, or initiative. However, in some cases, we go below the major program, office, or initiative level because of the diversity in federal agencies, their activities and data, and its relevance to critical sites. For example, EPA's Envirofacts Data Warehouse contains data from different major regulatory programs, such as Resource Conservation and Recovery Act (RCRA) and water discharge permit information.

Table B.1
Federal Geospatial Data Sources

Agency/ Suborganization	Title of Web Site for Program, Office, or Initiative	Location
Architect of the Capitol	**Architect of the Capitol Web Site**	**www.aoc.gov**
Capitol Visitor Center Project Office	Capitol Visitor Center—Overview	www.aoc.gov/cvc/cvc_ overview.htm
Central Intelligence Agency	**Central Intelligence Agency & Director of Central Intelligence**	**www.cia.gov**
Defense Nuclear Facilities Safety Board	**Defense Nuclear Facilities Safety Board**	**www.dnfsb.gov**
Department of Agriculture (USDA)	**United States Department of Agriculture's Home Page**	**www.usda.gov**
Agricultural Marketing Service	AMS at USDA—AMS Food Purchase Resources—Main Menu	www.ams.usda.gov/cp/
	AMS at USDA, Fruit and Vegetable Programs, Fresh Product Standards and Quality Certification	www.ams.usda.gov/fv/ fpbdigimage.html
	Auditing Services	www.ams.usda.gov/lsg/ arc/audit.htm
	Livestock and Grain Reports	www.ams.usda.gov/lsg/ mncs/index.htm
	AMS at USDA—Science and Technology—Pesticide Data Program	www.ams.usda.gov/ science/pdp/index.htm
	Grain Transportation Report Homepage	www.ams.usda.gov/ tmd/grain.htm
Agricultural Research Service	USDA-ARS Hydrology and Remote Sensing Laboratory	http://hydrolab.ars usda.gov
Animal and Plant Health Inspection Service	Animal and Plant Health Inspection Service (APHIS)	www.aphis.usda.gov
	CAHM [Center for Animal Health Monitoring] Home Page	www.aphis.usda.gov/ vs/ceah/cahm/index. htm

Table B.1—Continued

Agency/ Suborganization	Title of Web Site for Program, Office, or Initiative	Location
USDA (cont.)		
Animal and Plant Health Inspection Service (cont.)	Plant Protection and Quarantine	www.aphis.usda.gov/ ppq/
	Emergency Management Response System (EMRS)	www.aphis.usda.gov/vs /ep/emrs.html
Cooperative State Research, Education, and Extension Service	Cooperative State Research, Education, and Extension Service (CSREES) of USDA	www.reeusda.gov
Economic Research Service	ERS/USDA Data	www.ers.usda.gov/ Data/
Farm Service Agency	Farm Service Agency— US Department of Agriculture (USDA-FSA)—Entry Page	www.fsa.usda.gov
	Aerial Photography Field Office Home Page	www.apfo.usda.gov
	Welcome to the Farm Service Agency—Commodity Operations	www.fsa.usda.gov/ daco/default.htm
Food Safety Inspection Service	Office of Policy, Program Development and Evaluation Home Page	www.fsis.usda.gov/ OPPDE/op/
	OPHS [Office of Public Health and Science] Home Page	www.fsis.usda.gov/ OPHS/ophshome.htm
	TSC [Technical Service Center] Home Page	www.fsis.usda.gov/ OFO/TSC/
Foreign Agricultural Service	U.S. Trade Internet System	www.fas.usda.gov/ ustrade/
Forest Service	USDA Forest Service— Caring for the Land and Serving People	www.fs.fed.us
	Fire and Aviation Management	www.fs.fed.us/fire/fire_ new/
	USDA Forest Service	www.fs.fed.us/aboutus /org_chart.shtml

Table B.1—Continued

Agency/ Suborganization	Title of Web Site for Program, Office, or Initiative	Location
USDA (cont.)		
Forest Service (cont.)	GIS Coverages [Roadless Areas]	www.roadless.fs.fed.us /documents/feis/data/ gis/coverages/index. shtml
	GIS [Wasatch-Cache National Forest GIS Page]	www.fs.fed.us/wcnf/ gis/
Grain Inspection, Packers, and Stock- yards Administration	Grain Inspection	www.usda.gov/gipsa/
National Agricultural Library	AgNIC System Engineer	www.agnic.org
National Agricultural Statistics Service	USDA-NASS, State Statistical Offices Home Page	www.usda.gov/nass/ sso-rpts.htm
	South Dakota Agricultural Statistics Service	www.nass.usda.gov/sd/
	USDA, NASS, Research Division	www.nass.usda.gov/ research/avhrr/avhrr mnu.htm
Natural Resources Conservation Service	Natural Resources Conservation Service	www.nrcs.usda.gov/
	USDA: NRCS: Geospatial Data Gateway: Home	www.lighthouse.nrcs. usda.gov/gateway/ gatewayhome.html
	National Resources Inventory: NRCS [National Resources Inventory]	www.nrcs.usda.gov/ technical/NRI/
	USDA-NRCS Soils & Soil Survey	www.statlab.iastate. edu/soils/nssc/
	Regional and State Offices: NRCS	www.nrcs.usda.gov/ about/organization/ regions.html
Office of Community Development	Rural Empowerment Zones and Enterprise Communities Inter- net Home Page	www.ezec.gov

Table B.1—Continued

Agency/ Suborganization	Title of Web Site for Program, Office, or Initiative	Location
USDA (cont.)		
Risk Management Agency	Welcome to the RMA Web	www.rma.usda.gov
Rural Development	USDA Rural Development— About Us	www.rurdev.usda.gov/ rd/
Rural Utilities Service	Rural Utilities Service	www.usda.gov/rus/
Department of Commerce (DOC)	**Department of Commerce Home Page**	**www.commerce.gov**
Bureau of Economic Analysis	Gross Domestic Product (GDP) and Other US Economic Data from the Bureau of Economic Analysis	www.bea.doc.gov
Bureau of Industry and Security (Bureau of Export Administration)	The Home Page of the Bureau of Industry and Security (Formerly Bureau of Export Administration)	www.bis.doc.gov
Bureau of the Census	Census Bureau Home Page	www.census.gov
	U.S. Census Bureau Geography Web Page	www.census.gov/geo/ www/index.html
	LandView Main Page	www.census.gov/geo/ landview/
International Trade Administration	International Trade Administration—Home Page	www.trade.gov
National Institute of Standards and Tech- nology	National Institute of Standards and Technology	www.nist.gov
National Oceanic and Atmospheric Administration	NOAA Home Page	www.noaa.gov
	Center for Operational Oceanographic Products and Services (CO-OPS) Homepage	www.co-ops.nos.noaa. gov
	NOAA Coastal Services Center	www.csc.noaa.gov

Table B.1—Continued

Agency/ Suborganization	Title of Web Site for Program, Office, or Initiative	Location
DOC (cont.)		
National Oceanic and Atmospheric Administration (cont.)	NOAA CSC Products	www3.csc.noaa.gov/CS Cweb/genericPage.asp? bin=10
	NOAA CoastWatch Central Operations Homepage	coastwatch.noaa.gov
	NCDC: National Climatic Data Center (NCDC)	www.ncdc.noaa.gov/ oa/ncdc.html
	National Data Buoy Center	www.ndbc.noaa.gov
	Geostationary Satellite Server	www.goes.noaa.gov
	U.S. DoC/NOAA/NOS/National Geodetic Survey	www.ngs.noaa.gov
	USDOC/NOAA/NESDIS/National Geophysical Data Center (NGDC) Home Page	www.ngdc.noaa.gov
	NOAA Fisheries	www.nmfs.gov
	NOAA's National Ocean Service	http://oceanservice. noaa.gov/
	National Virtual Data System	www.nvds.noaa.gov
	NOAA—National Weather Service	www.nws.noaa.gov
	Office of Coast Survey— Marine Chart Division	http://chartmaker.ncd. noaa.gov/mcd/
	About Us—CPRD	http://response.restora tion.noaa.gov/cpr/ aboutus/aboutus.html
	NOAA Office of Response and Restoration	http://response.restora tion.noaa.gov/index. html
Critical Infrastructure Assurance Office	CIAO Home Page	www.ciao.gov
National Technical Information Service	NTIS	www.ntis.gov

Table B.1—Continued

Agency/ Suborganization	Title of Web Site for Program, Office, or Initiative	Location
DOC (cont.)		
Patent and Trademark Office Database	United States Patent and Trademark Office Home Page	www.uspto.gov
STAT-USA Database	STAT-USA/Internet: Home Page	www.stat-usa.gov
Department of Defense (DoD)		
Aberdeen Proving Ground	Environmental Activities at J-Field, Aberdeen Proving Ground, Maryland (Hosted by DOE ANL)	http://web1.ead.anl. gov/jfield/
Army Corps of Engineers	Coastal and Hydraulics Laboratory	http://chl.wes.army.mil
	Welcome to www. evergladesplan.org	www.evergladesplan. org
	IWR Home Page	www.iwr.usace.army. mil
	Los Angeles District—Reservoir Regulation Station	www.spl.usace.army. mil/resreg/
	National Inventory of Dams	http://crunch.tec.army. mil/nid/webpages/nid. cfm
	Corps of Engineers Navigation Data Center (NDC) Maintaining Databases of Waterborne Commerce, Domestic Commercial Vessels, Port Facilities, Lock Facilities and Lock Operations, and Navigation Dredging Projects	www.wrsc.usace.army. mil/ndc/index.htm
	Where We Are—US Army Corps of Engineers	www.usace.army.mil/ where.html#State
	Rock Island District—U.S. Army Corps of Engineers	www.mvr.usace.army. mil

Table B.1—Continued

Agency/ Suborganization	Title of Web Site for Program, Office, or Initiative	Location
DoD (cont.)		
Army Corps of Engineers (cont.)	NIC—Navigation Information Connection	www.mvr.usace.army. mil/navdata/Default. htm
	Water Management Center	http://water.mvr.usace. army.mil
	USAED–St Paul Water Control Center Public Web Server	www.mvp-wc.usace. army.mil
	PCASE–Airfield Road Transportation Software (USACE Transportation Systems Center)	www.pcase.com/ screenshots.htm
	Airfield & Pavements Branch—Roads, Airfields, Railroads—Transportation Software	http://pavement.wes. army.mil
Army National Guard	Army National Guard—ARNG	www.arng.army.mil
Engineer Research and Development Center	Tri-Service Civil Works CADD/GIS/FM Registry and Clearinghouse	www.nww.usace.army. mil/apps/tscwrc/
Fort Belvoir	Welcome to the Fort Belvoir Home Page	www.belvoir.army.mil
Military Traffic Management Command	Military Traffic Management Command Transportation Engineering Agency (MTMCTEA)	www.tea.army.mil/ DATA/default.htm
National Imagery and Mapping Agency	NIMA	www.nima.mil
	NIMA: Aeronautical Information	https://164.214.2.62/pro ducts/digitalaero/index. html
	NIMA: Airfield Initiative Program	http://164.214.2.62/pro ducts/rbai/index.html
	Geospatial Engine	http://geoengine.nima. mil
	NIMA: (U) Geospatial Sciences Division (Unclassified)	http://164.214.2.59/ GandG/

Table B.1—Continued

Agency/ Suborganization	Title of Web Site for Program, Office, or Initiative	Location
DoD (cont.)		
National Imagery and Mapping Agency (cont.)	Digital Nautical Chart (DNC) Home Page (Maritime Safety Information Division)	www.nima.mil/cda/ article/0,2311,3104_ 12135_118824,00.html
National Reconnaissance Office	National Reconnaissance Office	www.nro.gov
Office of the Secretary of Defense	DefenseLINK—Official Web Site of the U.S. Department of Defense	www.defenselink.mil
Other DoD Installations	FY02 Base Structure Report	www.defenselink.mil/ news/Jun2002/base structure2002.pdf
United States Air Force	USAF GeoBase Information Portal	https://www.il.hq.af. mil/geobase/
	Environmental Management Virtual Tours	www.eglin.af.mil/em/ virtualtours/index.htm
	Base Map	http://web.archive.org/ web/20010131233500/ www.macdill.af.mil/ BaseMap.asp
United States Air Force Research Lab	The Air Force Research Laboratory Splash Page	www.afrl.af.mil
	Model Based Vision Library	www.mbvlab.wpafb. af.mil
United States Army	The United States Army Homepage	www.army.mil
United States Navy	U.S. Navy Office of the Information	www.chinfo.navy.mil
Department of Energy (DOE)	**U.S. Department of Energy Home Page**	**www.doe.gov**
Alternative Fuels Data Center	Alternative Fuels Data Center Home	www.afdc.doe.gov
Ames National Laboratory	Ames Laboratory Home Page	www.external.ames lab.gov/

Table B.1—Continued

Agency/ Suborganization	Title of Web Site for Program, Office, or Initiative	Location
DOE (cont.)		
Argonne National Lab	Argonne National Laboratory Home Page	www.anl.gov
	ANL-West—Home Page	www.anlw.anl.gov
Bonneville Power Marketing Administration	Bonneville Power Administration	www.bpa.gov/ corporate/kc/home/ index.cfm
Brookhaven National Laboratory	Brookhaven National Laboratory	www.bnl.gov/world/
	BNL Environmental Restoration Division	www.bnl.gov/erd/
	Waste Management Division	www.bnl.gov/wmd/
Carlsbad Field Office	WIPP [Waste Isolation Pilot Plant] Home Page	www.wipp.carlsbad. nm.us/
Departmental Representative to the DNFSB [Defense Nuclear Facilities Safety Board]	Facility Representative Home	www.facrep.org
Energy Efficiency and Renewable Energy Network	Distributed Energy Resources Home	www.eere.energy.gov/ der/
	U.S. Department of Energy Building Technologies Program Home Page	www.eere.energy.gov/ buildings/index.cfm
Energy Information Administration	Energy Information Administration Home Page	www.eia.doe.gov
	U.S. Energy Information Administration: Office of Coal, Nuclear, Electric and Alternate Fuels	www.eia.doe.gov/ cneaf/
	Coal Home Page	www.eia.doe.gov/ fuelcoal.html
	Electricity Home Page	www.eia.doe.gov/ fuelelectric.html

Table B.1—Continued

Agency/ Suborganization	Title of Web Site for Program, Office, or Initiative	Location
DOE (cont.)		
Energy Information Administration (cont.)	Notice to Readers	www.eia.doe.gov/ emeu/reps/eimap/ei_ contents.html
Environmental Measurements Laboratory	EML: Environmental Measurements Laboratory	www.eml.doe.gov
Federal Energy Regulatory Commission	Federal Energy Regulatory Commission	www.ferc.gov
Fermi National Research Laboratory	Fermi National Accelerator Laboratory	www.fnal.gov
Grand Junctions Office	U.S. Department of Energy Grand Junction Office (Long-Term Surveillance and Maintenance Program)	http://lts1.gjo.doe.gov
Idaho National Engineering and Environmental Laboratory	Idaho National Engineering and Environmental Laboratory	www.inel.gov
	Environmental Monitoring— INEEL	www.inel.gov/environ ment/monitoring/
Independent Oversight and Performance Assurance Office	DOE Independent Oversight and Performance Assurance Program	www.oa.doe.gov
Lawrence Berkeley National Lab	Lawrence Berkeley National Laboratory	www.lbl.gov
National Energy Technology Laboratory	Strategic Center for Natural Gas—National Energy Technology Laboratory	www.netl.doe.gov/ scng/
National Nuclear Security Administration	National Nuclear Safety Administration	www.nnsa.doe.gov
National Renewable Energy Laboratory	National Renewable Energy Laboratory (NREL) Home Page	www.nrel.gov

Table B.1—Continued

Agency/ Suborganization	Title of Web Site for Program, Office, or Initiative	Location
DOE (cont.)		
National Renewable Energy Laboratory (cont.)	Wind Energy Resource Atlas of the United States	http://rredc.nrel.gov/wind/pubs/atlas/
National Spent Nuclear Fuel Program	Welcome to the National Spent Nuclear Fuel Program Home Page	http://nsnfp.inel.gov
National Transportation Program	TRAGIS	http://apps.ntp.doe.gov/tragis/tragis.htm
Nevada Field Operations Office	DOE/NA—U.S. Department of Energy Nevada Site Office	www.nv.doe.gov/Default.htm
Oak Ridge National Laboratory	Oak Ridge National Laboratory (Oak Ridge ORNL Science Technology Transfer Research Development)	www.ornl.gov
	Geographic Information Science & Technology, ORNL	www.ornl.gov/gist/gisthome.html
	ORNL ESD GIS Facility Homepage	http://wag21.esd.ornl.gov
Oak Ridge Operations Office	Oak Ridge Operations— US Department of Energy	www.oakridge.doe.gov
Office of Civilian Radioactive Waste Management	OCRWM—Office of Civilian Radioactive Waste Management	www.ocrwm.doe.gov
Office of Environmental Management	U.S. Department of Energy Office of Environmental Management (EM)	www.em.doe.gov/index4.html
Office of Fissile Materials Disposition	Function: Threat Reduction	www.nn.doe.gov/functions_threat.shtml
Office of Fossil Energy	DOE Fossil Energy— Natural Gas Regulation	www.fe.doe.gov/oil_gas/im_ex/
	DOE-Fossil Energy: Strategic Petroleum Reserve Storage Sites	www.fe.doe.gov/spr/site_descriptions/spr_sites.html

Table B.1—Continued

Agency/ Suborganization	Title of Web Site for Program, Office, or Initiative	Location
DOE (cont.)		
Office of Nuclear Energy, Science and Technology	Office of Nuclear Energy, Science and Technology—DOE	www.ne.doe.gov
Ohio Field Office	The Ohio Field Office	www.ohio.doe.gov
Pacific Northwest National Laboratory	Pacific Northwest National Laboratory	www.pnl.gov
	NorthWest Infrared (Remote Sensing and Electro Optics)	https://secure.pnl.gov/ nsd/NSD.nsf/Welcome? OpenForm
Richlands Operations Office	Environmental Restoration Projects	www.bhi-erc.com/ projects/
Sandia National Laboratories	Sandia National Laboratories	www.sandia.gov/ Main.html
	Transportation Risk & Packaging at Sandia National Laboratories	http://ttd.sandia.gov/ risk/gis.htm
Southwestern Power Marketing Administration	Southwestern Power Marketing Administration	www.swpa.gov/index. html
Stanford Linear Accelerator Center	Welcome to SLAC (Stanford Linear Accelerator Center)	www.slac.stanford.edu
Thomas Jefferson National Accelerator Facility	Thomas Jefferson National Accelerator Facility	www.jlab.org
Thomas Jefferson National Accelerator Facility	Integrated Emergency Management	www.jlab.org/intralab/ emergency/
Western Area Power Marketing Administration	Western Area Power Administration Home Page	www.wapa.gov
Yucca Mountain Site Office	Yucca Mountain Project Home Page	www.ymp.gov
Department of Health and Human Services (DHHS)	**United States Department of Health and Human Services**	**www.hhs.gov**

Table B.1—Continued

Agency/ Suborganization	Title of Web Site for Program, Office, or Initiative	Location
DHHS (cont.)		
Administration for Children and Families	Administration for Children and Families Home Page	www.acf.dhhs.gov
Agency for Healthcare Research and Quality	Agency for Healthcare Research and Quality (AHRQ) Home Page	www.ahrq.gov
Center for Medicare and Medicaid Services (HCFA deprecated)	Centers for Medicare & Medicaid Services (Formerly HCFA)	www.hcfa.gov
Centers for Disease Control and Prevention	Centers for Disease Control and Prevention	www.cdc.gov
	ATSDR—Agency for Toxic Substances and Disease Registry/U.S. Dept. of Health and Human Services	www.atsdr.cdc.gov
	Division of Public Health Surveillance and Informatics	www.cdc.gov/epo/ dphsi/
	Chronic Disease Prevention	www.cdc.gov/nccdphp/
	National Center for Environmental Health	www.cdc.gov/nceh/ ncehhome.htm
	National Center for Health Statistics	www.cdc.gov/nchs/
	National Center for Infectious Diseases	www.cdc.gov/ncidod/
	National Center for Injury Prevention and Control Home Page	www.cdc.gov/ncipc/
	NIP [National Immunization Program]: Public Home Page	www.cdc.gov/nip/
	NIOSH—The National Institute for Occupational Safety and Health	www.cdc.gov/niosh/ homepage.html

Table B.1—Continued

Agency/ Suborganization	Title of Web Site for Program, Office, or Initiative	Location
DHHS (cont.)		
Centers for Disease Control and Prevention (cont.)	NIOSH Mining Safety and Health Research	www.cdc.gov/niosh/ mining/
Food and Drug Administration	Office of Regulatory Affairs Start Page on the FDA Web	www.fda.gov/ora/
Health Resources and Services Administra- tion	HRSA [Health Resources and Services Administration]	www.hrsa.gov
Indian Health Service	Indian Health Service— About IHS	www.ihs.gov
National Institutes of Health	National Institutes of Health (NIH)	www.nih.gov
Substance Abuse and Mental Health Services Administration	The Substance Abuse & Mental Health Services Administration SAMHSA	www.samhsa.gov
Department of Housing and Urban Develop- ment (HUD)	**Homes and Communities— U.S. Department of Housing and Urban Development (HUD)**	**www.hud.gov**
Office of Multifamily Housing Programs	Office of Multifamily Housing Programs—HUD	www.hud.gov/offices/ hsg/hsgmulti.cfm
Policy Development and Research	Welcome to HUD USER— Policy Development and Research's Information Service	www.huduser.org
Department of Justice (DOJ)		
Drug Enforcement Agency	Drug Enforcement Administration Home	www.usdoj.gov/dea/ index.htm
Federal Bureau of Investigation	Federal Bureau of Investigation Home Page	www.fbi.gov
Federal Bureau of Prisons	BOP Home Page	www.bop.gov

Table B.1—Continued

Agency/ Suborganization	Title of Web Site for Program, Office, or Initiative	Location
DOJ (cont.)		
Immigration and Naturalization Service	USINS INS Internet Home Page	www.ins.usdoj.gov/ graphics/index.htm
National Archive of Criminal Justice Data	Access Data	www.icpsr.umich.edu/ NACJD/archive.html
Office of Justice Programs	Bureau of Justice Statistics Crime & Justice Data Online	http://149.101.22.40/ dataonline/Search/ Crime/Crime.cfm
	Mapping Tools	www.ojp.usdoj.gov/ cmrc/
	Crime Mapping Research Center Homepage	www.icpsr.umich.edu/ ORG/Publications/ NACJD/nij2000.pdf
	Office for Domestic Pre- paredness Homepage	www.ojp.usdoj.gov/ odp/
United States Attorney Offices	U.S. Attorneys' Offices	www.usdoj.gov/usao/ offices/index.html
United States Marshals Service	U.S. Marshals Service— District Offices	www.usdoj.gov/ marshals/usmsofc.html
Department of Labor (DOL)		
Bureau of Labor Statistics	At a Glance Tables	www.bls.gov/eag/ home.htm
	Geographic Profile of Employment and Unem- ployment Home Page	www.bls.gov/gps/ home.htm
Department of State (DOS)	**US Department of State: Home Page**	**www.state.gov**
Bureau of Intelligence and Research	Bureau of Intelligence and Research	www.state.gov/s/inr/
International Boundary and Water Crossings	Home	www.ibwc.state.gov

Table B.1—Continued

Agency/ Suborganization	Title of Web Site for Program, Office, or Initiative	Location
DOS (cont.)		
Office of Protocol	Office of Protocol	www.state.gov/s/cpr/
U.S. Embassies	U.S. Dept of State FOIA [Freedom of Information Act] Electronic Reading Room	www.foia.state.gov/ mms/KOH/keyofficers. asp
Department of the Interior (DOI)	**Department of the Interior**	**www.doi.gov**
Bureau of Indian Affairs	This Website Is Temporarily Unavailable	www.doi.gov/bureau-indian-affairs.html
Bureau of Land Management	BLM AML Inventory Page—Link to AMLS [Abandoned Mine Lands Information System]	www.blm.gov/aml/ amlis.htm
	Bureau of Land Management National Web Page (Alaskan Regional Office)	www.ak.blm.gov
	BLM Arizona—Lake Havasu Field Office GPS Maps	www.az.blm.gov/gps/ gps.htm
	Download GCDB Data	www.ca.blm.gov/ cadastral/readme.html
	BLM Colorado—Browse Page	www.co.blm.gov/ browse/browse_2_13. htm
	BLM-ES Home Page (Eastern States Regional Office)	www.es.blm.gov/
	Home—BLM GLO [General Land Office] Records	www.glorecords.blm. gov
	GeoCom Explorer	www.geocommuni cator.gov/explorer
	Land Survey Information System	www.lsi.blm.gov/ website/lsi/viewer.htm? Title=Land%20Survey %20Information
	Geospatial Support Team	www.blm.gov/gis/
	Idaho Bureau of Land Management	www.id.blm.gov

Table B.1—Continued

Agency/ Suborganization	Title of Web Site for Program, Office, or Initiative	Location
DOI (cont.)		
Bureau of Land Management (cont.)	WIS [Well Information System] Home Page	www.wispermits.org
	BLM Montana/Dakotas Home Page	www.mt.blm.gov
	NARSC [National Applied Resource Sciences Center] GIS	www.blm.gov/gis/ narsc/
	National Landscape Con- servation System Map	www.blm.gov/nlcs/ map.htm
	BLM Public Lands & Administrative Jurisdictions	www.blm.gov/nstc/ jurisdictions/
	Mineral Materials DB	http://158.68.233.67/ minerals.nsf?Open Database
	Nevada BLM Home	www.nv.blm.gov
	BLM, New Mexico, Oklahoma, Kansas, Texas	www.nm.blm.gov
	BLM Oregon/Washington State Office: Home Page	www.or.blm.gov
	Information Resources Management/GIS Website— BLM, Oregon/Washington	www.or.blm.gov/gis/ index.asp
	GCDB [Geographic Coordinate Data Base] National Home Page (Public Land Survey System: Cadastral Survey)	www.blm.gov/gcdb/
	BLM Utah Home Page	www.ut.blm.gov
	GIS (Mapping Sciences)	www.ut.blm.gov/geo sciences/mappingsci/ gis.html
	Bureau of Land Management Wyoming	www.wy.blm.gov
Bureau of Reclamation	Bureau of Reclamationtion [sic] Home Page	www.usbr.gov

Table B.1—Continued

Agency/ Suborganization	Title of Web Site for Program, Office, or Initiative	Location
DOI (cont.)		
Bureau of Reclamation (cont.)	Bureau of Reclamation Hydropower Program	www.usbr.gov/power/
	USBR RSGIS Archive Library	www.rsgis.do.usbr.gov/ html/archives.html
	Water Operations Information Within the Bureau of Recla- mation	www.usbr.gov/main/ water/
	Great Plains Region— Bureau of Reclamation	www.gp.usbr.gov
	Bureau of Reclamation— Lower Colorado Region	www.usbr.gov/lc/ region/
	Welcome to the Mid-Pacific Region Homepage	www.mp.usbr.gov/
	U.S. Department of the Interior—National Irrigation Water Quality Program	www.usbr.gov/niwqp/ index.html
	Bureau of Reclamation (Pacific Northwest Region)	www.usbr.gov/pn/
	Upper Colorado Region, US Bureau of Reclamation: Home Page	www.uc.usbr.gov/wrg/ index.html
U.S.–Mexico Border Field Coordinating Committee	DOI Field Cooridinating Committe [sic] Home Page	www.cerc.usgs.gov/fcc/
Fish and Wildlife Service	Environmental Conservation Online System	http://ecos.fws.gov
	GIS—U.S. Fish and Wildlife Service (Information Resources Management: National Data Administration Office)	www.fws.gov/data/ gishome.html
	Migratory Bird Data Center Home Page	http://birddata.fws.gov
	National Wetlands Inventory Home Page	http://wetlands.fws.gov

Table B.1—Continued

Agency/ Suborganization	Title of Web Site for Program, Office, or Initiative	Location
DOI (cont.)		
Fish and Wildlife Service (cont.)	U.S. Fish & Wildlife Service: Southwest Region 2	http://southwest.fws.gov
	Welcome to the Great Lakes–Big Rivers Region	www.midwest.fws.gov
	Region 4: U.S. Fish and Wildlife Service Home	http://southeast.fws.gov
	North Carolina Endangered and Threatened Species	http://nc-es.fws.gov/es/es.html
	Welcome to the Northeast Region, U.S. Fish and Wildlife Service	http://northeast.fws.gov/
	Region 6, the Mountain-Prairie Region, U.S. Fish and Wildlife Service	http://mountain-prairie.fws.gov/
	USFWS Alaska: Alaska Region	www.r7.fws.gov
	U.S. Fish and Wildlife Service, Pacific Region	www.r1.fws.gov
Mineral Management Service	MMS Home Page	www.mms.gov
	Minerals Revenue Management Home Page	www.mrm.mms.gov
	Offshore Minerals Management Home Page	www.mms.gov/offshore/
	Minerals Management Service—Alaska Region Homepage	www.mms.gov/alaska/
	Minerals Management Service—Gulf of Mexico Region Homepage	www.gomr.mms.gov/index.html
	POCSR Home Page	www.mms.gov/omm/pacific/
National Park Service	National Park Service—Experience Your America	www.nps.gov

Table B.1—Continued

Agency/ Suborganization	Title of Web Site for Program, Office, or Initiative	Location
DOI (cont.)		
National Park Service (cont.)	GIS—National Park Service Geographic Information Systems (GIS)	www.nps.gov/gis/
	National Archeological Database: MAPS	www.cast.uark.edu/ other/nps/maplib/
	CRGIS Community Base Station (Cultural Resources Mapping & GIS)	www2.cr.nps.gov/gis/ basestation/index.htm
	Inventory of Historic Light Stations—Summary List by State (Marine Heritage Program)	www.cr.nps.gov/ maritime/ltsum.htm
	National Historic Landmarks Program (NHL)	http://tps.cr.nps.gov/ nhl/
	Using the NRIS—National Register of Historic Places Research Page	www.cr.nps.gov/nr/ research/nris.htm
	National Trails System: Home (National Center for Recreation & Conservation)	www.ncrc.nps.gov/ programs/nts/index. html
	Species in Parks: Flora and Fauna Databases (Information Center for the Environment— ICE)	http://ice.ucdavis.edu/ nps/
Office of Surface Mining	Office of Surface Mining Home Page	www.osmre.gov
	Office of Surface Mining Applicant/Violator System Office Website	www.avs.osmre.gov
	Mine Map Repository Home Page	mmr.osmre.gov
United States Geological Survey	Home Page of the USGS Atlas of Antarctic Research	http://usarc.usgs.gov/ antarctic_atlas/
	NBII Clearinghouse Search (National Coal Resources Data System)	http://mercury.ornl. gov/nbii/

Table B.1—Continued

Agency/ Suborganization	Title of Web Site for Program, Office, or Initiative	Location
DOI (cont.)		
United States Geological Survey (cont.)	Center for Integration of Natural Disaster Information (CINDI) Index Page	http://cindi.usgs.gov
	Noga Online—Choose a Map	http://certmapper.cr. usgs.gov/noga/servlet/ MapWindowServ
	EarthExplorer	http://edcsns17.cr.usgs. gov/EarthExplorer/
	USGS ESIC: Earth Science Information Centers	http://mapping.usgs. gov/esic/esic_index. html
	USGS GEO-DATA Explorer	http://dss1.er.usgs.gov
	USGS Mapping Information: Geographic Names Information System (GNIS)	http://geonames.usgs. gov
	USGS Geologic Information— Maps	http://pubs.usgs.gov/ products/maps/
	Earth Science Data on the Global Land Information System	http://edcwww.cr.usgs. gov/webglis/
	USGS: Maps on Demand	http://rockyweb.cr.usgs. gov/mod/index.html
	Digital Raster Graphics	http://mcmcweb.er. usgs.gov/drg/
	U.S. Geological Survey: Mineral Resources On-Line Spatial Data	http://mrdata.usgs.gov/ index.html
	EarthExplorer Map Finder (Photofinder/NAPP)	http://edcwww.cr.usgs. gov/Webglis/glisbin/ finder_main.pl?dataset _name=NAPP
	National Atlas of the United States	http://nationalatlas.gov /natlas/natlasstart.asp
	US COALQUAL Database Introduction (National Coal Resources Data System)	http://energy.er.usgs.g ov/products/databases/ CoalQual/intro.htm

Table B.1—Continued

Agency/ Suborganization	Title of Web Site for Program, Office, or Initiative	Location
DOI (cont.)		
United States Geological Survey (cont.)	USGS National Geologic Map Database (National Cooperative Geologic Mapping Program)	http://ngmdb.usgs.gov
	USGS Geography Informational Home Page	http://mapping.usgs.gov/
	EROS Data Center, Sioux Falls, SD	http://edc.usgs.gov/geodata/
	USGS EDC: National Elevation Dataset Home Page	http://edcnts12.cr.usgs.gov/ned/
	GISDATA Map Studio	http://gisdata.usgs.net
	USGS Topographic Maps Home Page	http://mcmcweb.er.usgs.gov/topomaps/
	Gateway to the Earth: Project/NAWQA Program	http://orxddwimdn.er.usgs.gov/servlet/page?_pageid=543&_dad=portal30&_schema=PORTAL30
	USGS Rocky Mountain Mapping Center	http://rockyweb.cr.usgs.gov
	TerraServer Homepage	http://terraserver.homeadvisor.msn.com/default.asp
	USGS Geography: The National Map	http://nationalmap.usgs.gov
	USGS—Water Resources of the United States (Water Resources Division)	http://water.usgs.gov
	Current USGS Streamgage Network	http://water.usgs.gov/nsip/nsipmaps/currentgages.html
	Ground-Water Data for the Nation (National Water Inventory System)	http://waterdata.usgs.gov/nwis/gw

Table B.1—Continued

Agency/ Suborganization	Title of Web Site for Program, Office, or Initiative	Location
DOI (cont.)		
United States Geological Survey (cont.)	Water-Quality Data for the Nation (National Water Inventory System)	http://waterdata.usgs. gov/nwis/qw
	Surface-Water Data for the Nation (National Water Inventory System)	http://waterdata.usgs. gov/nwis/sw
	USGS Drinking Water Programs (Office of Water Quality)	http://water.usgs.gov/ owq/dwi/
	USGS Water Resources Applications Software	http://water.usgs.gov/ software/
	Digital Orthophoto Quadrangles	www-wmc.wr.usgs. gov/doq/
	Geopubs—USGS Western Region Geological Publications	http://geopubs.wr.usgs. gov
Department of Transportation (DOT)		
Bureau of Trans- portation Statistics	2001 National Transportation Atlas Data	http://websas.bts.gov/ website/ntad/main download.html
	BTS—Geographic Information Services (2001 National Transportation Atlas Data: Transportation Facilities)	www.bts.gov/gis/ ntatlas/facilities.html
	National Transportation Data Archive (NTDA)	www.bts.gov/ntda/
	USDOT: BTS: NTL: TRIS Online	http://199.79.179.82/ sundev/search.cfm
	BTS—Airline Information	www.bts.gov/oai/
Federal Aviation Administration	FAA—FAA Home Page	www.faa.gov
	FAA—AIS—Cartographic Standards—Obtaining Aeronautical Charts	www.faa.gov/nfdcata 100/130/130obta.html

Table B.1—Continued

Agency/ Suborganization	Title of Web Site for Program, Office, or Initiative	Location
DOT (cont.)		
Federal Aviation Administration (cont.)	The National Aviation Safety Data Analysis Center	http://nasdac.faa.gov
	Notices to Airmen	www1.faa.gov/ntap/ SPECIALNOTAMS/
	Federal Aviation Admini- stration Office of Accident Investigation	www.faa.gov/avr/aai/ iirform.htm
	ASD 400—Investment Analysis and Operations Research	www1.faa.gov/asd/ ia-or/
	Commercial Space Transportation—FAA/AST	http://ast.faa.gov
	Commercial Space Transportation—FAA/AST (Operations at Towered Airports)	http://ast.faa.gov
	Aviation Information	http://av-info.faa.gov
	Runway Safety	www.faarsp.org
	National Aeronautical Charting Office—NACO (Aviation System Standards)	www.naco.faa.gov
Federal Highway Administration	Central Federal Lands Highway Division	www.cflhd.gov
	Eastern Federal Lands Highway Division	www.efl.fhwa.dot.gov
	National Scenic Byways Online	www.byways.org
	Highway Performance Monitoring System (HPMS—Office of Highway Policy Information—FHWA)	www.fhwa.dot.gov/ ohim/hpmspage.htm
	Office of Highway Policy Information Home Page	www.fhwa.dot.gov/ ohim/
	Office of Safety Home Page	http://safety.fhwa.dot. gov

Table B.1—Continued

Agency/ Suborganization	Title of Web Site for Program, Office, or Initiative	Location
DOT (cont.)		
Federal Motor Carrier Safety Administration	A&I [Analysis and Information Online]	http://ai.volpe.dot.gov/ mcspa.asp
	National Hazardous Material Route Registry	http://hazmat.fmcsa. dot.gov/
	SAFER Web	www.safersys.org/ CSP_Order.asp
	Federal Motor Carrier Safety Administration—Performance and Registration Information Systems	www.fmcsa.dot.gov/ factsfigs/prism.htm
Federal Railroad Administration	Automated Track Inspection Program	http://atip.ensco.com
	FRA Office of Safety Homepage	http://safetydata.fra. dot.gov/OfficeofSafety/
Federal Transit Administration	Welcome to the National Transit Database	www.ntdprogram.com/ NTD/ntdhome.nsf? OpenDatabase
Maritime Administration	Office of Ship Operations	www.marad.dot.gov/ Offices/Ship/
	Office of Statistical & Economic Analysis	www.marad.dot.gov/ statistics/usfwts/
National Highway Traffic Safety Administration	NHTSA—National Highway Traffic Safety Administration	www.nhtsa.dot.gov
	NCSA—Available Information	www-nrd.nhtsa.dot. gov/departments/nrd- 30/ncsa/TextVer/CID. html
	NCSA—State Data System	www-nrd.nhtsa.dot. gov/departments/nrd- 30/ncsa/SDS.html
Research and Special Programs Administration	OET/TEM Transportation Emergency Management	www.rspa.dot.gov/oet/

Table B.1—Continued

Agency/ Suborganization	Title of Web Site for Program, Office, or Initiative	Location
DOT (cont.)		
Research and Special Programs Administration (cont.)	Contact Information	http://ops.dot.gov
	Welcome to the Hazmat Safety Home Page	http://hazmat.dot.gov
Saint Lawrence Seaway Development Corporation	Great Lakes St. Lawrence Seaway System: Seaway Map	www.greatlakes- seaway.com/en/seaway map/index.html
Surface Transporta- tion Board	Surface Transportation Board—Home Page	www.stb.dot.gov
Transportation Security Admini- stration	TSA—Transportation Security Administration	www.tsa.gov/trav_ consumers/airports. shtm
United States Coast Guard	POISE Contains Maritime	www.uscg.mil/ safeports/
	MSO Mobile—Local Marine Safety Information Bulletin Page	www.uscg.mil/d8/ mso/mobile/Gstrp/ mainGSTRP.htm
	National Response Center: Intro Page	www.nrc.uscg.mil
	DGPS General Information— USCG Navigation Center	www.navcen.uscg.gov/ dgps/default.htm
	Vessel Response Plans	www.e-vrp.com
Environmental Protec- tion Agency (EPA)	**Environmental Protection Agency**	**www.epa.gov**
	EPA Geospatial Data— Theme-Based Browse	www.epa.gov/nsdi/pag es/theme_browse.html
Clean Air Markets Program	EPA's Clean Air Markets— The Emissions & Generation Resource Integrated Database	www.epa.gov/air markets/egrid/index. html

Table B.1—Continued

Agency/ Suborganization	Title of Web Site for Program, Office, or Initiative	Location
EPA (cont.)		
Envirofacts Data Warehouse (cont.)	EPA—Envirofacts—BRS Query	www.epa.gov/enviro/ html/brs/brs_query. html
	EPA—Envirofacts—Overview	www.epa.gov/enviro/ html/ef_overview.html
	EPA—Envirofacts—Multisystem Query	www.epa.gov/enviro/ html/multisystem_ query_java.html
	EPA—Envirofacts Warehouse— PCS—Water Discharge Permits Query Form	www.epa.gov/enviro/ html/pcs/pcs_query_ java.html
	EPA—Envirofacts—RCRAInfo— Query Form	www.epa.gov/enviro/ html/rcris/rcris_query_ java.html
	EPA—Window to My Environment	www.epa.gov/enviro/ wme/
	EnviroMapper	http://maps.epa.gov/ enviromapper/
Environmental Monitoring and Assessment Program	US EPA—Environmental Monitoring and Assessment Program (EMAP)	www.epa.gov/docs/ emap/index.html
Facility Registry Service	EPA—Envirofacts—FRS— Query Form	www.epa.gov/enviro/ html/fii/fii_query_java. html
National Center for Environmental Assessment	National Center for Envi- ronmental Assessment— Risk Models and Tools	http://cfpub.epa.gov/ ncea/cfm/ncearisk models.cfm?ActType= DatabaseAndTools& detype=model&exc Col=Archive
National Health and Environmental Effects Research Laboratory	Mid-Atlantic Inventory— The National Environmental Monitoring Initiative	www.epa.gov/ cludygxb/site-mid.html

Table B.1—Continued

Agency/ Suborganization	Title of Web Site for Program, Office, or Initiative	Location
EPA (cont.)		
Office of Air and Radiation	EPA-OAQPS Enhanced Ozone Monitoring—PAMS—PAMS Networks and Sites	www.epa.gov/air/ oaqps/pams/network. html
	EPA AIRNow	www.epa.gov/airnow/
	AIRS Executive for Windows	www.epa.gov/airs/ aewin/index.html
	EPA AirData—Access to Air Pollution Data	www.epa.gov/air/data/ index.html
Office of Environmental Information	EQ Environmental Atlas	www.epa.gov/ceis web1/ceishome/atlas/
Office of Pesticide Programs	EPA: Pesticides—Pesticide Data Submitters List (PDSL)	www.epa.gov/ opppmsd1/Data SubmittersList/
	NPIRS: National Pesticide Information Retrieval System	http://ceris.purdue.edu/ npirs/index.html
Office of Solid Waste	Wastes: Municipal Solid Waste Landfills	www.epa.gov/epa oswer/non-hw/muncpl/ landfill/index.htm#list
Office of Water	EPA WATERS Homepage	www.epa.gov/waters/
	National Drinking Water Contaminant Occurrence Database	www.epa.gov/ncod/
	Environmental Protection Agency—Local Drinking Water Information	www.epa.gov/ogwdw/ dwinfo.htm
	Environmental Protection Agency (Accessing EPA's Drinking Water Data in SDWIS/FED)	www.epa.gov/safe water/data/getdata. html
	The Safe Drinking Water Information System/State Version (SDWIS/State)	www.epa.gov/safe water/sdwis_st/state. htm

Table B.1—Continued

Agency/ Suborganization	Title of Web Site for Program, Office, or Initiative	Location
EPA (cont.)		
Office of Water (cont.)	About BASINS 3.0—U.S. EPA	www.epa.gov/water science/basins/basinsv3. htm
	EPA Clean Watersheds Needs Survey (CWNS)	www.epa.gov/owm/ uc.htm
	EPA: National Estuary Program: Which Estuaries Are in the NEP?	www.epa.gov/owow/ estuaries/find.htm
Region 10 Office	Environmental Protection Agency—Region 10 GIS Map Library	www.epa.gov/r10 earth/maplib.html
Region 2 Office	GIS Data by Geographic Area	www.epa.gov/region 02/gis/data/thematic data.htm
Region 4 Office	GIS—Geographic Information Systems	www.epa.gov/Region4/ gis/index.html
Region 5 Office	U.S.E.P.A.—Region 5— R.M.D.—O.I.S.—Download	www.epa.gov/reg5 ogis/download/index. htm
Region 6 Office	EPA Region 6 Geographic Information System	www.epa.gov/ Arkansas/6en/gis/
Region 7 Office	EPA Region 7—GIS	www.epa.gov/region7/ envdata/gis/gis.html
Region 8 Office	Region 8 GIS Data Inventory	www.epa.gov/Region8/ gis/gisdata.html
Region 9 Office	San Gabriel Valley GIS Data	www.epa.gov/Region9/ waste/sfund/npl/ sangabriel/gisdata.html
STORET (Storage and Retrieval)	EPA: Water: Wetlands, Oceans, & Watersheds: Monitoring and Assessing Water Quality: STORET	www.epa.gov/storet/
Superfund Program	Superfund Information Systems: CERCLIS Hazardous Waste Sites	www.epa.gov/super fund/sites/cursites/ index.htm

Table B.1—Continued

Agency/ Suborganization	Title of Web Site for Program, Office, or Initiative	Location
EPA (cont.)		
Superfund Program (cont.)	NPL Sites in the US, NPL, Superfund, US EPA	www.epa.gov/super fund/sites/npl/npl.htm
Surf Your Watershed	EPA: Surf Your Watershed: Locate Your Watershed	http://cfpub.epa.gov/ surf/locate/index.cfm
Toxics Release Inventory	Toxics Release Inventory (TRI) Program	www.epa.gov/tri
Watershed Information Network Atlas	EPA: Watershed Information Network: Watershed Atlas	www.epa.gov/water atlas/
Export-Import Bank	**Export-Import Bank of the United States**	**www.exim.gov**
Federal Communications Commission (FCC)		
Wireless Telecommunications Bureau	FCC: ULS Databases	http://wireless.fcc.gov/ cgi-bin/wtb-datadump. pl
	FCC Universal Licensing System (ULS)	http://wireless.fcc.gov/ uls/
	FCC Universal Licensing System (ULS) (Antenna Structure Registration System)	http://wireless.fcc.gov/ antenna/
	TOWAIR Determination	http://wireless2.fcc.gov/ UlsApp/AsrSearch/ towairSearch.jsp
Federal Emergency Management Agency (FEMA)	**Federal Emergency Management Agency**	**www.fema.gov**
Federal Insurance and Mitigation Administration	FEMA: Flood Hazard Mapping	www.fema.gov/mit/tsd/
Mapping and Analysis Center	FEMA: ITS—2001 Maps	www.gismaps.fema. gov/2001pages/2001 maps.shtml

Table B.1—Continued

Agency/ Suborganization	Title of Web Site for Program, Office, or Initiative	Location
FEMA (cont.)		
Map Service Center	FEMA: Map Service Center	http://msc.fema.gov/ MSC/product.htm
National Dam Safety Program	FEMA: National Dam Safety Program	www.fema.gov/fima/ damsafe/
National Fire Incident Reporting System	USFA—NFIRS—National Fire Incident Reporting System	www.nfirs.fema.gov/ nfirs_userlogin.htm
Regional Offices	FEMA: Regional and Area Offices	www.fema.gov/about/ regoff.htm
U.S. Fire Administration	USFA—Hotel-Motel National Master List	www.usfa.fema.gov/ hotel/state_download. cfm
Winter Storm Update Center	FEMA: Winter Storm Update Center	www.fema.gov/fema/ wsuc.htm
General Services Administration	**GSA Home**	**www.gsa.gov**
Public Buildings Service	Public Buildings Service	http://hydra.gsa.gov/ pbs/
	Welcome to the Retail Tenant Services Center of Expertise!	http://hydra.gsa.gov /pbs/centers/retail/
Interagency/Other		
EPA/NOAA	Get CAMEO	www.epa.gov/ swercepp/cameo/ request.htm
FDIC	FDIC: Individual Banks	www.fdic.gov/bank/ individual/index.html
Federal Reserve Bank	Board of Governors of the Federal Reserve System	www.federalreserve. gov
	Financial Report Search (Federal Reserve National Information Center)	http://132.200.33.161/ nicSearch/servlet/NIC Servlet?GRP=FINREP T&REQ=BHC&MODE= SEARCH

Table B.1—Continued

Agency/Suborganization	Title of Web Site for Program, Office, or Initiative	Location
Interagency/Other (cont.)		
FedStats.gov	FedStats: MapStats	http://www.fedstats.gov/qf/
Federal Geographic Data Committee	Federal Geographic Data Committee	http://130.11.52.184/
FirstGov	FirstGov—The U.S. Government's Official Web Portal	www.firstgov.gov/
Mid-Atlantic Integrated Assessment Project	Mid-Atlantic Integrated Assessment Project	http://md.water.usgs.gov/maia/
National Fire Plan	National Fire Plan	www.fireplan.gov/fire_maps.cfm
National Interagency Coordination Center	National Interagency Coordination Center	www.nifc.gov/news/nicc.html
National Interagency Fire Center	GeoMAC [Geospatial Multi-Agency Coordination]—Wildland Fire Support	http://geomac.usgs.gov
NBII	The National Biological Information Infrastructure (NBII) Home Page	www.nbii.gov
Recreation.gov	Recreation.gov	www.recreation.gov/aboutrecgov.cfm
Regional Ecosystem Office	Northwest Forest Plan Regional Ecosystem Office	www.reo.gov
Security and Exchange Commission	SEC Filings & Forms (EDGAR)	www.sec.gov/edgar.shtml
Library of Congress (LOC)	**The Library of Congress**	**www.loc.gov**
American Memory/Historical Collections	LC HABS/HAER Collections Search	http://memory.loc.gov/ammem/hhquery.html
Center for Geographic Information	Geography and Map Division Homepage, Library of Congress	www.loc.gov/rr/geogmap/

Table B.1—Continued

Agency/ Suborganization	Title of Web Site for Program, Office, or Initiative	Location
National Aeronautics and Space Administration (NASA)	NASA—Welcome	www.nasa.gov
Earth Observatory	EO Observation Deck: View Dataset Holdings	http://earth observatory.nasa.gov/ Observatory/datasets. html
	NASA's Visible Earth	http://visibleearth.nasa. gov
Earth Science Enterprise	Earth Science Image Studio and Multimedia	http://earth.nasa.gov/ Introduction/studio. html
Goddard Space Flight Center	EOS Data Gateway at redhook.gsfc.nasa.gov	http://redhook.gsfc. nasa.gov/~imswww/ pub/imswelcome/plain. html
Human Spaceflight	Human Space Flight (HSF)— Orbital Tracking	http://spaceflight.nasa. gov/realdata/tracking/ index.html
Jet Propulsion Laboratory	Shuttle Radar Topography Mission	www.jpl.nasa.gov/srtm/ dataprod.htm
Johnson Space Center	Earth from Space	http://earth.jsc.nasa. gov
Headquarters	NASA Environmental Management Division: GIS	www.hq.nasa.gov/ office/codej/codeje/je_ site/gis/about_gis.html
	The Disaster Finder	http://disasterfinder. gsfc.nasa.gov
Imagery Exchange	NASA Image eXchange (NIX)	http://nix.nasa.gov
National Archives and Records Administration	NARA: US National Archives & Records Administration	www.nara.gov
National Science Foundation (NSF)	National Science Foundation (NSF)—Home Page	www.nsf.gov
Ocean Sciences	NSF GEO Division of Ocean Science	www.geo.nsf.gov/oce/

Table B.1—Continued

Agency/ Suborganization	Title of Web Site for Program, Office, or Initiative	Location
NSF (cont.)		
WOCE: World Ocean Circulation Experiment (Texas A&M)	U.S. WOCE Home Page	www-ocean.tamu.edu/ WOCE/uswoce.html
Nuclear Regulatory Commission	**NRC: Home Page**	**www.nrc.gov**
Electronic Reading Room	NRC: Document Collections	www.nrc.gov/reading-rm/doc-collections/
Enforcement Program	NRC: Current Issues and Actions	www.nrc.gov/what-we-do/regulatory/ enforcement/current. html#reactor
Office of Nuclear Material Safety and Safeguards	NRC: Office of Nuclear Material Safety and Safeguards	www.nrc.gov/who-we-are/organization/ nmssfuncdesc.html
Office of Nuclear Reactor Regulation	NRC: Office of Nuclear Reactor Regulation	www.nrc.gov/who-we-are/organization/ nrrfuncdesc.html
Office of Nuclear Security and Incident Response	NRC: Office of Nuclear Security and Incident Response	www.nrc.gov/who-we-are/organization/nsirfu ncdesc.html
Supreme Court of the United States	**Supreme Court of the United States**	**www.supremecourt us.gov**
Tennessee Valley Authority (TVA)	**TVA: Home Page**	**www.tva.gov**
Environmental Stewardship	TVA: Environmental Stewardship	www.tva.com/ environment/
Map Store	TVA Map & Photo Records	www.tva.gov/river/ mapstore/index.htm
River System Operations and Environment	TVA: River Information	http://lakeinfo.tva.gov
Transmission and Power Supply	TVA: Power Home Page	www.tva.gov/power

Table B.1—Continued

Agency/ Suborganization	Title of Web Site for Program, Office, or Initiative	Location
United States International Trade Commission	**U.S. International Trade Commission**	**www.usitc.gov**
United States Treasury	**United States Department of the Treasury—Home**	**www.treas.gov**
Bureau of Alcohol, Tobacco, and Firearms	ATF Online—Bureau of Alcohol, Tobacco, Firearms and Explosives	www.atf.treas.gov
Comptroller of the Currency, Administrator of National Banks	OCC—Comptroller of the Currency, Administrator of National Banks	www.occ.treas.gov
Federal Financial Institutions Examination Council	FFIEC Home Page	www.ffiec.gov
Office of Thrift Supervision	Office of Thrift Supervision	www.ots.treas.gov
U.S. Customs Service	U.S. Customs Service	www.customs.ustreas. gov
U.S. District Courts	**The Federal Judiciary**	**www.uscourts.gov**

Detailed Examples of Geospatial Information Analyses

We presented the general observations and conclusions from our geospatial information analyses in Chapter Three. This appendix discusses detailed examples of four databases that we concluded to be of potentially medium significance in providing relatively more detailed and unique geospatial information relevant to particular types of U.S. critical infrastructure facilities. In addition, we briefly discuss one of the other in-depth case studies not already discussed in Chapter Three.

Databases of Medium Significance

The Department of Transportation and the Nuclear Regulatory Commission

Of the 629 federal databases examined, we found four that appeared to have *medium* significance. These four databases have been either withdrawn since 9/11 or were password-protected since then.

At the Department of Transportation Research and Special Programs Administration, we identified two databases that looked potentially significant: the Office of Pipeline Safety's Pipeline Risk Management/Integrity Management Database and the Office of Pipeline Safety's National Pipeline Mapping System. Ranking conservatively and using the limited information describing these databases caused us to classify them as medium significance. However, we were unable to examine the databases directly because of password restriction; so an extensive evaluation might change such a ranking.

The third database identified as having medium significance was the Nuclear Regulatory Commission's (NRC's) Office of Nuclear Reactor Regulation Plant Information Books detailing U.S. nuclear facilities, which the agency had previously placed on the Web before they were withdrawn following 9/11. We could not directly view this database because it was not even found on a Web archive site. Based on the description of this site and the fact that it contained detailed information about nuclear facilities' internal workings, we ranked it as having medium significance for targeting usefulness. We identified a few alternatives for the detailed technical information it likely contained. For example, the Natural Resources Defense Council, an environmental NGO, publishes a book on nuclear weapons manufacturing that includes extensive technical information about the internal workings of the facilities.[1] Given that the alternatives for this NRC's database were low and our team's targeting feedback medium, the site was considered as having medium significance.

The fourth example, U.S. Bureau of Reclamation's DataWeb site, we describe more in depth below.

U.S. Bureau of Reclamation's DataWeb: The Grand Coulee Dam

The Department of the Interior (DOI) Bureau of Reclamation's DataWeb online mapping Web site also was ranked as having medium significance, although the site was withdrawn from public access after 9/11. Prior to the attacks, the Web site provided detailed technical information for dam community users, such as industry and universities, containing comprehensive case files and records of its dams and activities.

When examining this database, we used the Grand Coulee Dam as our case study. The detailed engineering information on the dam could conceivably be useful to potential attackers, both for choosing the target and helping plan an attack. Most of the detailed technical

---

[1] Cochran (1987).

information is not traditional geospatial information but rather operational information about internal features and functions of the dam.

In searching for alternative sources for this type of information, we found that such sources exist but with differing levels of content. However, most of the alternatives did not have as much or as specific detailed information (e.g., internal features and functions) on the dam, so the alternatives were ranked as *low*.

We found federal, state, and local government; NGO; international; and individual sources with alternative information, most which contained more general information than that found on the DataWeb source yet widely available due to Grand Coulee's public nature. Since the facility is a well-known tourist destination, general information was not difficult to find. Table C.1 provides specific examples of alternative sources for two types of general information: location and information about the importance of the facility (such as the fact that it is the largest hydroelectric energy generation facility in the United States). Other federal sources included the U.S. Army Corps of Engineers and The Federal Emergency Management Agency's Dam Safety Program; state and local government sources included the Grand Coulee Chamber of Commerce and Washington state; and national and international NGOs included the Association of Dam Safety Officials, the U.S. and International Committee on Large Dams, and the World Commission on Dams. Even individuals' Web sites provided some interesting more detailed information related to internal features, such as a biking enthusiast's site that provided pictures and details about his bike ride and visit to the dam, as well as a Grand Coulee Dam enthusiast who provided pictures of internal features.

We ranked DataWeb as having medium potential significance to attackers because it contains potentially useful information (i.e., medium usefulness) and because the alternative sources were ranked *low*, since detailed data were available but limited and harder to obtain.

Table C.1
Federal and Nonfederal Data Source Comparison for U.S. Bureau of
Reclamation's DataWeb: The Grand Coulee Dam

Data Element at Federal Site	Nonfederal Alternative Source Providing the Same Data
General location: zip code, area map, etc.	Grand Coulee Dam Area Chamber of Commerce informational Web site
	Grand Coulee Dam Software, commercial Web site
	Center Lodge Motel, Grand Coulee, Wash.
	Mapquest.com imagery
Description or photographs of internal facilities	Grand Coulee Dam enthusiast
	Bicycling enthusiast's national tour—personal photography
Importance of the facility: information about capacity and size, fact that it is the largest hydroelectric energy generation facility in the United States	Go Northwest! travel guide
	Amazon.com books on the dam (and various other literature and reports detailing its development)
	World Commission on Dams (and other various dam associations)

Other In-Depth Case Studies

We looked at 11 federal geospatial databases as in-depth case studies in which a specific critical site was identified within the federal database:

- DOI Bureau of Reclamation's DataWeb: The Grand Coulee Dam
- DOI MMS: Houchin offshore mining platform (discussed in Chapter Three)

- HUD: E-MAPS/Marcus Hook oil refinery² (discussed in Chapter Three)
- NOAA nautical charts: Calvert Cliffs, Maryland, nuclear plant
- Nuclear Regulatory Commission (NRC) non-power/research reactors
- Tennessee Valley Authority: Environmental Impact Statement for Brown's Ferry nuclear plant
- U.S. Army Corps of Engineers: Los Angeles Reservoir Dam inundation maps
- U.S. EPA Biennial Reporting System (BRS): Milan, Tennessee, Army Ammunition Plant
- U.S. EPA TRI: Marcus Hook oil refinery (discussed in Chapter Three)
- USGS: DOQ/MacDill Air Force Base, Florida
- USGS: topographic maps for different infrastructure at Grand Teton National Park and Yellowstone National Park.

As mentioned in Chapter Three, we selected these cases to cover a range of geospatial information types (e.g., DOQ image, map, and textual document containing geospatial information) and potential target types (e.g., dam, nuclear facility, military base, energy facility, ammunition plant) with an emphasis on what was viewed as more sensitive sites and information types. For example, DOI representatives had concerns about the public accessibility of inundation maps, so we chose one as a case study example. We also tried to complement what was already being studied in the targeting assessment—i.e., the demand analysis.

We briefly discuss another in-depth case study, the U.S. EPA Biennial Reporting System (BRS), since it illustrates an analytic tool capability.

---

² We explored the Marcus Hook facility for two different federal databases—HUD E-MAPS and EPA TRI—to examine the relationships between different federal sources that provide the same information. Namely, E-MAPS uses TRI data and combines it with other information, potentially adding more value to it, such as providing additional analytical capability.

U.S. EPA Biennial Reporting System: Milan, Tennessee, Army Ammunition Plant

The 1976 federal Resource Conservation and Recovery Act for hazardous waste established that EPA collect industry hazardous waste information in the BRS and that it be public information. For selected facilities that use and process large volumes of hazardous materials, the database contains detailed information about the tons of hazardous waste processed and where the material goes, by chemical names. Contact names and addresses are also provided for both the facility and waste sites. Communities, NGOs, and other interested individuals use this public information for emergency planning, to provide accountability regarding such hazardous materials, and for other public purposes.

The BRS data are easily accessible by anyone, in a variety of formats. Besides Web access at the BRS site, the information is also available at EPA's Envirofacts data warehouse, in CD-ROM form, and in hard-copy documents.

One of the most interesting features of the BRS online database is its capabilities as an analytical tool. The user can quickly and easily search the database for multiple facility information and see the volume of hazardous materials at the different facilities. Within a few minutes, we searched an OSHA list of Standard Industrial Classification codes and found the one for ammunition plants. We entered the code into this BRS Web site and were thus able to determine that the Milan, Tennessee, Army ammunition plant has processed extremely large volumes of hazardous materials and to identify where the plant sent its waste for disposal.

This information appeared potentially useful for an attacker's information needs. However, such data are at least two years old before they become available. In addition, we found that there are numerous alternative sources that provide information on the Milan plant, many of which provide more detailed and potentially more useful information.

Since the facility is a public-private partnership, many promotional facility, plant manager, and industry group Web sites provide detailed information on the Milan plant. Industry Web sites, such as

General Dynamics and American Ordnance, mostly make available installation marketing materials about the plant's capabilities. For example, Operation Enterprise (see Openterprise.com) has detailed plant statistics (number of buildings, square footage, basic utility information, etc.). Commercial aerial image warehouses provide images of this facility, as do federal agencies, such as the USGS PhotoFinder. In turn, there are several other federal information sources for this plant. USDA's Retooling program (ARMS) provides basic contact information for the plant. DoD facility information sources included the Army Operation Support Command and the DoD DefenseLINK base listing.

Further, NGOs and private individuals had plant information that was readily accessible via the Web. For example, GlobalSecurity. org posts the environmental remediation plan for the Milan facility, including a rough map layout, pictures of buildings at the facility, and site information about hazardous wastes. Interestingly, we found conceivably more useful information—the CSXT train route schedule and radio communication frequencies—on an individual train enthusiast's Web site.

In conclusion, this database was ranked as having low potential significance to an attacker because, while it is potentially useful to help the attacker choose a target (i.e., medium), many other sources with more detailed data were also available, limiting the database's uniqueness.

Overview of Critical U.S. Sites: Critical Infrastructure and Other Key Homeland Locations

This appendix provides an overview of critical U.S. sites that could be potential targets of attack by terrorist groups or hostile governments. In this report, we define critical sites to include the following range of facilities and locations within the U.S. homeland:

- critical infrastructure facilities and structures
- other key assets of national importance
  —locations of cultural significance
  —military installations
  —locations where large population gatherings occur.

The aim of this appendix is to provide a general assessment of the potential vulnerability of critical U.S. sites by focusing on two key dimensions of the problem: (1) the diverse nature of U.S. facilities and structure, both among the different categories above and within each category, and (2) the degree of public accessibility that is available for different types of critical sites. Such distinctions are relevant to this report because they provide insights on the opportunities that potential attackers have for collecting relevant information through direct access to, or direct observation of, various key sites throughout the country. This appendix examines these questions by taking a closer look at the energy sector as a critical infrastructure protection problem and certain types of other key assets.

Critical Sites: Accessibility and Potential Vulnerability

For potential attackers, such as terrorist groups, seeking to cause casualties or economic disruption, the United States is a "target-rich environment." Many critical sites are relatively vulnerable to various types of attacks involving conventional explosives, weapons of mass destruction, or unconventional means of attack, such as aircraft crashes. As a recent U.S. government report on physical protection of critical infrastructures notes:

> Our Nation's critical infrastructures and key assets are a highly complex, heterogeneous, and interdependent mix of facilities, systems, and functions that are vulnerable to a wide variety of threats. Their sheer numbers, pervasiveness, and interconnected nature create an almost infinite array of high-payoff targets for terrorist exploitation.[1]

These vulnerabilities arise from a variety of factors, including the nature of many facilities and structures as well as the fact that most critical sites are relatively accessible to the public and thus particularly vulnerable to various types to attackers. While increased security measures were instituted at many critical sites (e.g., airports, bridges, tunnels, train stations) following 9/11, public access to a majority of such locations cannot be fundamentally curtailed without imposing unacceptable social and economic costs.

To improve the protection of the most critical facilities and locations within the U.S. homeland, the federal government is pursuing a comprehensive national approach to their physical and cyber protection in partnership with state and local governments and the private sector. A key element of this strategy is developing comprehensive, multitier protection policies and programs[2] that are likely to incorporate information protection policies to ensure that potential attackers are denied access to sensitive information on critical facilities and locations, including geospatial information.

---

[1] The White House (2003, p. 2).

[2] The White House (2003, p. 16).

An important aspect of this protection strategy is the ensuring of federal government access to what is being defined as "critical" infrastructure information, which is information that is mostly generated by private-sector companies and is not usually in the public domain for infrastructure security purposes. The legislation that created DHS also contains provisions that protect the voluntary sharing of critical infrastructure information between the private sector and federal agencies by exempting such information from disclosure under the Freedom of Information Act.[3]

Critical U.S. Infrastructure

Critical infrastructure is a broad term and has evolved over time. For the purposes of this study, critical infrastructure encompasses the 13 sectors presented in Table D.1, which correspond to the updated categories defined by the U.S. National Strategy.[4] The critical infrastructure sectors consist of the diverse systems and assets most integral to the operations of the national defense and the U.S. economy. A majority of these assets are owned and operated by the private sector. Although distinct sectors have been identified, in fact, the U.S. critical infrastructure has evolved into a highly interdependent and dynamic network in recent years, adding to its potential vulnerability to physical and cyber attackers. This table lists examples of the diverse U.S. critical sites, as well as our general assessment of their relative degree of public accessibility.

Establishing a Spectrum of Information "Sensitivity"

The complex and constantly evolving quality of most critical infrastructures, and the wide range of facilities and systems the term encompasses, can make it difficult to make precise determinations

---

[3] See Homeland Security Act of 2002 (Section 214).

[4] See The White House (2003, p. 6).

Table D.1
U.S. Critical Infrastructure Sectors

Sector	Example Assets	Degree of Public Accessibility
Agriculture	• Grain storage elevators	Medium to substantial
Food	• Meat processing plants	Medium to substantial
Water	• Drinking water facilities	Substantial
	• Dams	Limited to substantial
Public health	• Hospitals	Substantial
	• National pharmaceutical stockpiles and supplies	Limited
Emergency services	• Emergency operations centers	Medium to substantial
Government	• Government agency headquarters	Limited to medium
	• Regional offices	Medium to substantial
Defense industrial base	• Military equipment manufacturing plants	Medium to substantial
Information and telecommunications	• Transmission sites	Medium
	• Internet backbone facilities	Medium to substantial
Energy	• Nuclear power plants	Limited to medium
	• Oil refineries	Limited to medium
Transportation	• Bridges	Substantial
	• Tunnels	Substantial
	• Pipelines	Substantial
Banking and finance	• Major financial exchanges	Substantial
	• Financial utilities	Medium
Chemical industry and hazardous materials	• Chemical processing plants	Limited to medium
	• Hazmat material transportation	Medium to substantial
Postal and shipping	• Mail processing centers	Medium to substantial

about their potential exploitability. Clearly, not all infrastructures generate information that is vital or volatile. After all, the "sensitivity" of publicly available information varies depending on the accessibility of the site. The more accessible and open the site, the less sensitive additional information on the site becomes. Inversely, the less accessible or closed the site, the more sensitive information on the site becomes. As discussed in Chapter Two, the level of accessibility greatly influences the information needs of the attackers. Returning to our three categories of site accessibility presented in Figure 2.1—public, limited, and restricted—we can create a spectrum from low to high sensitivity for all associated information.

Information relating to the first category of sites, *publicly accessible* locations, has the lowest level of sensitivity because low-risk opportunities for direct observation exist for potential attackers. Information on the second category of accessibility, *limited* access sites, has varying levels of sensitivity. Other than external observation, fewer alternatives exist to obtain more specific information on the locations. Finally, information for *restricted* access sites has a very high degree of sensitivity because of the very limited number of alternative information sources. Since U.S. critical sites have few targets within restricted access, direct access and direct observation by potential attackers become viable options for collecting information needed for planning an attack.

Identifying Potentially Sensitive Information by Critical Infrastructure

Having considered information sensitivity based on the level of access, we factor in a consideration of *kinds* of infrastructure information available. As might be expected, the range of publicly available information sources on critical infrastructure is extremely diverse. The various sectors of critical infrastructure sectors have unique types of facilities, structures, and locations. Consequently, information that is potentially sensitive will vary by sector (e.g., agricultural, transportation), by type of site (e.g., factory, hospital, power plant), and among similar sites in different locations (e.g., urban vs. rural).

Aggregating critical infrastructure by sector and representative facility type provides a context for examining how the three categories of accessibility vary within overall critical infrastructure. Some sectors, such as agriculture, are almost completely publicly accessible while other sectors, such as energy, have a higher number of limited access locations. Still other critical infrastructure sectors, such as transportation, have hybrid sites that include publicly accessible locations (e.g., airports) that have limited access components (e.g., control towers). Government is virtually the only critical infrastructure sector with highly restricted access locations.

As an example of how accessibility can vary substantially within a critical infrastructure sector, we examine the diversity of types of facilities and structures associated with the energy sector, which consists of two main components: electrical power systems and oil and natural gas.

Energy Sector

Electrical Power Systems

Electrical power systems are complex networks composed of the generation, transmission, control, and support networks, which work together to supply electricity to end users. Overall, the national electrical power grid is an extremely interconnected and dynamic system. It is comprised of more than 3,000 utilities and rural cooperatives. The major electrical power generation sources are coal, nuclear, hydroelectric, gas, and petroleum. The generation systems can include steam turbines, diesel engines, and hydraulic turbines. Transmission networks are the means of electricity transfer from generators to end users. Control networks are the information control points that regulate overall system operations. Support networks provide resources and information that the other networks need to operate.

Energy Sector: Oil and Natural Gas

Oil and natural gas supplies more than 60 percent of U.S. energy consumption.[5] This high level is in large part because oil and natural gas energy encompass a wide range of applications, from electric

---

[5] National Petroleum Council (2001, p. 4).

power generation to automobiles, and is composed of a range of fuel types, including crude and refined petroleum, petroleum-derived fuels (e.g., kerosene), and natural gas (e.g., liquid, compressed). Production, storage, and transportation components make up the oil and natural gas critical infrastructure. The production component of oil and natural gas relates to fuel extraction from underground sources—for example, through drilling facilities and recovery fields. The processing component includes refining and processing facilities. The transportation and storage component consists of the physical means of transfer—through pipelines, ships, rails, and storage in fuel tanks. Additionally, such information networks as SCADA (Supervisory Control and Data Acquisition) regulate overall system operations. As with the electrical power system, one can see the multiple components at work, each involving facilities, networks, and multiple nodes at which access considerations could come into play.

Vulnerabilities

The potential vulnerabilities of the energy sector vary significantly with regard to possible impact within and outside its systems. Vulnerabilities exist in terms of both physical and cyber attack. In general terms, the targets of potential highest value are those located in populated rural or urban areas where attacks will generate the greatest prospective impact. In addition, energy-sector facilities that contain hazardous materials, of which there are many, could also prove vulnerable targets. Targets meeting both of these criteria should be considered as highly vulnerable.

Most facilities in the energy sector tend to fall into the *limited access* category of sites. These facilities include

- Electrical Power Systems
    —*generation facilities*, such as nuclear power plants, fossil fuel plants, and many hydroelectric dams
    —*control networks*, including control centers
    —*support networks*, such as information systems like SCADA network hardware and the transportation and storage of fuel essential to power generation such as fuel storage sites

- Oil and Natural Gas
  —*production facilities*, such as drilling platforms and fields
  —*processing and storage facilities*, including oil refineries, gas plants, and storage tanks
  —*information control networks*, such as SCADA system network hardware.

Such high-value facilities tend to have limited public access because they are locations where the general public is usually not authorized to be and often have at least a minimal degree of security measures, including fences or barriers to make unauthorized entry difficult as well as access controls and security personnel. There are, however, some important types of critical infrastructure facilities and transportation assets in the energy sector that are *publicly accessible*.

- Electrical Power Systems
  —*transmission networks*, such as transformers, microwave communication towers, and transmission substations
- Oil and Natural Gas Facilities
  —*transportation mechanisms*, including pipelines, compressor stations, ports, rail lines, ships, and trucks.

Thus, this examination of the energy sector illustrates the diversity of its subcomponents and the varying degrees of public access associated with these critical sites.

Other Key Assets

The range of critical U.S. infrastructure sites is vast but not all-inclusive of potential homeland vulnerabilities. Homeland locations that are not components of the critical infrastructure sectors may also be at risk of attack by terrorists or other adversaries. Other key assets do exist besides the critical infrastructure sectors. As noted earlier, these assets generally fall into three types of sites: (1) locations of cultural significance, (2) special event locations, and (3) military installations. We assess their relative degree of accessibility in Table D.2 and the following paragraphs:

- *Locations of cultural significance* encompass virtually all locations that are recognizable as national symbols. These sites can include monuments, landmarks, buildings, and other structures that uniquely represent a national or regional characteristic of America. Most of these locations feature a high degree of public access, such as the Lincoln Memorial, St. Louis Arch, Seattle Space Needle, and various national parks.
- *Special event locations* primarily apply to sites of large population gatherings that occur regularly or sporadically. Examples include major sporting events, such as the Super Bowl, World Series, Olympic Games, World Cup, or other major public events, such as the New Year's Eve celebration in New York City's Times Square or Fourth of July celebrations in large cities across the country, including the Washington Mall. Other events that can feature large gatherings of population include religious gatherings and large entertainment events or simply large commercial business establishments (e.g., shopping centers during seasonal peaks). Although perimeter security is increasingly a feature at some of these locations where large population gathering occur, such as the Super Bowl, these venues are fundamentally accessible to well-organized attackers that could exploit the vulnerability through disguised ground attacks or attacks from above using aircraft or standoff weapons.
- *Military installations* represent a special category of critical sites that largely have limited public access. These relatively numerous sites are dispersed around the U.S. homeland in a wide range of urban, suburban, and rural locations. Particularly since 9/11, public access to military installations has been severely curtailed. On the other hand, most military installations rely on a wide array of commercial services to perform routine support services as a result of a continuing trend toward outsourcing nonessential activities. As a result, access restrictions may vary.

Table D.2
Relative Public Accessibility to Key Assets

Locations	Examples	Relative Degree of Public Accessibility
Locations of cultural significance	• Historical locations • National monuments • National parks	Substantial Substantial Substantial
Large population gatherings	• Major sporting or entertainment events • National celebrations • Commercial centers	Medium to substantial Medium to substantial Medium to substantial
Military installations	• The Pentagon • Army installations • Air Force bases • Navy installations	Low to medium Low to medium Low to medium Low to high

Furthermore, some military installations, such as the Pentagon and some U.S. naval surface fleet areas can be observed through drive-by vehicles or local boat traffic. Finally, private aircraft and helicopters could be used for fly-by observation of at least the facilities located near the periphery of these military installations.

Summary

This overview highlights the diversity of facilities that comprise the nation's critical infrastructure, as well as certain other key locations (e.g., cultural landmarks, military installations) that could be the target of attacks by terrorist groups or others. One particularly useful way of categorizing these disparate critical sites is to consider what degree of accessibility they permit to potential adversaries seeking information for targeting purposes. Many facilities (e.g., rail stations, bridges, hospitals) are highly accessible to the public and, therefore, to such potential attackers. This direct access greatly enhances the attacker's opportunities for acquiring the types of information needed for attack planning purposes. In comparison, most other critical infrastructure facilities limit public access mainly to individuals (e.g., workers, customers, government representatives) with appropriate credentials. However, in many cases, potential attackers would have the capability to undertake various forms of surveillance on such facilities, either through ground-level reconnaissance or even aerial overflights or flybys. Thus, the degree of public accessibility of different types of U.S. critical sites is likely to influence the information requirements of potential attackers, including their degree of interest in publicly available geospatial information sources.

Bibliography

Baker, John C., Kevin M. O'Connell, and Ray A. Williamson, eds., *Commercial Observation Satellites: At the Leading Edge of Global Transparency*, Santa Monica, Calif.: RAND Corporation and the American Society for Photogrammetry and Remote Sensing, MR-1229, 2001.

Bernhardsen, Tor, *Geographic Information Systems: An Introduction*, 2nd edition, New York: John Wiley & Sons, 1999.

Cochran, Thomas B., William M. Arkin, Robert S. Norris, and Milton M. Hoenig, *Nuclear Weapons Databook Series Volume III: U.S. Nuclear Warhead Facility Profiles*, New York: Harper & Row, 1987.

Eversole, John, "For Responders' Sake, Retain Hazmat Placarding," *Homeland Protection Professional*, November/December 2002, p. 12.

Fischer, Steven, and Samuel Hall, "US National Mapping System Growing, Adjusting to Security Concerns," *Oil & Gas Journal*, November 26, 2001, pp. 68–72.

Foresman, Timothy W., ed., *The History of Geographic Information Systems: Perspectives from the Pioneers*, Upper Saddle River, N.J.: Prentice Hall PTR, 1998.

Francica, Joe, "MapQuest.com Serves Maps to the Masses," *Business Geographics*, May 2000.

Frost & Sullivan, *World Remote-Sensing Data and GIS Software Markets*, Mountain View, Calif., 1999.

Georgia GIS Data Clearinghouse, "About the Clearinghouse." Online at www.gis.state.ga.us/Clearinghouse/clearinghouse.html (accessed January 2004).

"Geospatial One-Stop," *Federal Geographic Data Committee Newsletter*, Vol. 6, No. 1, Winter 2002.

Gillespie, Stephen R., *GIS Technology Benefits: Efficiency and Effectiveness Gains*, U.S. Geological Survey, Reston, Va., 1994a.

_____, "Measuring the Benefits of GIS Use: Two Transportation Case Studies," *URISA Journal*, Vol. 6, No. 2, Fall 1994b.

_____, "A Model Approach to Estimating GIS Benefits," unpublished article, U.S. Geological Survey, Reston, Va., 1997.

Guzy, Gary S., "Are We Protecting Secrets or Removing Safeguards?" *Washington Post*, November 24, 2002.

Hammond, Mark, "Business Mapping Helps Companies Make the Right Moves," *eWEEK*, January 29, 1999.

Homeland Security Act of 2002. Online at www.dhs.gov/interweb/ assetlibrary/hr_5005_enr.pdf (accessed December 2003).

Lachman, Beth E., "Public-Private Partnerships for Data Sharing: A Dynamic Environment," Santa Monica, Calif.: RAND Corporation, DRU-2259-NASA/OSTP, April 2000.

Lachman, Beth E., Anny Wong, Debra Knopman, and Kim Gavin, *Lessons for the Global Spatial Data Infrastructure: International Case Study Analysis*, Santa Monica, Calif.: RAND Corporation, DB-380-USGS, 2002.

Longmore-Etheridge, Ann, "Refined Protection," *Security Management*, August 2002, pp. 45–51.

Lowe, Jonathan W., "Maps in Motion: Spatial Data on Mobile Devices," *Geospatial Solutions*, June 2000.

McInnis, Logan, and Stuart Blundell, "Analysis of Geographic Information Systems (GIS) Implementations in State and County Governments of Montana," prepared for the Montana Geographic Information Council, Helena, Mont., October 1998.

McKee, Lance, "Local Governments Benefit from 'Open' Web Mapping," *GEOWorld*, August 2000.

Meisner, Sue, "NIMA Joins with USGS and FGDC to Form National Coalition for Geospatial Assurance," *The Edge*, November 2001, pp. 12–13.

Montana State Library, "Natural Resource Information System." Online at http://nris.state.mt.us/gis/default.htm (accessed December 2003).

NAPA—*see* National Academy of Public Administration.

National Academy of Public Administration, *Geographic Information for the 21st Century*, Washington, D.C., January 1998.

National Institute of Standards and Technology, Information Technology Laboratory, Computer Security Division, *Standards for Security Categorization of Federal Information and Information Systems*, initial public draft, Gaithersburg, Md.: U.S. Department of Commerce, Technology Administration, National Institute of Standards and Technology, Federal Information Processing Standards Publication FIPS 199, 2003.

National Petroleum Council, *Securing Oil and Natural Gas Infrastructures in the New Economy*, June 2001.

National Research Council, *The Future of Spatial Data and Society: Summary of a Workshop*, Washington, D.C.: National Academy Press, 1997.

New York State Library, "New York State GIS Clearinghouse." Online at www.nysgis.state.ny.us (accessed December 2003).

O'Brien, Kevin, "Open Sources Closed Since 9/11," *Jane's Intelligence Review*, February 2002, p. 2.

Office of Management and Budget, *Circular A-16, Revised,* The Executive Office of the President, Washington, D.C., August 19, 2002. Online at www.whitehouse.gov/omb/circulars/a016/a016_rev.html (accessed December 2003).

OMB—*see* Office of Management and Budget.

Oxford Economic Research Associates, *The Economic Contribution of Ordnance Survey GB*, Oxford, UK, September 24, 1999.

Pace, Scott, David Frelinger, Beth E. Lachman, Arthur C. Brooks, and Mark David Gabriele, *The Earth Below: Purchasing Science Data and the Role of Public-Private Partnerships*, Santa Monica, Calif.: RAND Corporation, DB-316-NASA/OSTP, 2000.

Pace, Scott, Kevin M. O'Connell, and Beth E. Lachman, *Using Intelligence Data for Environmental Needs: Balancing National Interests*, Santa Monica, Calif.: RAND Corporation, MR-799-CMS, 1997.

Pace, Scott, Brant Sponberg, and Molly Macauley, *Data Policy Issues and Barriers to Using Commercial Resources for Mission to Planet Earth*, Santa Monica, Calif.: RAND Corporation, DB-247-NASA/OSTP, 1999.

Parrish, Jay, "High-Resolution Imagery Trends," *Imaging Notes*, Fall 2003, pp. 16–17.

"Post-9/11, 'Sanitized' Sites Aim to Shield Data, Agencies, Groups Remove Information Deemed Too Sensitive," *CNN.com*, September 10, 2002.

Reginster, Yves, "ETeMII: Integrating GI into the Information Society," 4th Global Spatial Data Infrastructure Conference, Cape Town, South Africa, March 13–15, 2000.

Report of the Independent Commission on the National Imagery and Mapping Agency, *The Information Edge: Imagery Intelligence and Geospatial Information in an Evolving National Security Environment*, December 2000.

Report of the President's Commission on Critical Infrastructure Protection, *Critical Foundations: Protecting America's Infrastructures*, October 1997.

Riley, Jack K., et al., *California's Vulnerability to Terrorism*, Santa Monica, Calif.: RAND Corporation, MR-1430-OES (government distribution only), 2002.

Robb, Drew, "GPS Finds Its Place," *Government Computing News*, July 1, 2000.

Rubenstein, Ed, "Chains Chart Their Courses of Actions with Geographic Information Systems," *Nation's Restaurant News*, February 9, 1998.

Ryan, Barbara J., "One Year After: A USGS Perspective," *Geospatial Solution*, September 2002, pp. 56–57.

Sommers, Rebecca, *Framework: Introduction and Guide*, Federal Geographic Data Committee, Washington, D.C., 1997.

_____, "Framework Data Survey: Preliminary Report," *GeoInfo Systems* (supplement), September 1999.

Texas Association of Counties, "GIS Helps Kerr County Add Property to Tax Rolls," *County*, Vol. 11, No. 4, July/August 1999a.

_____, "Smart Maps Improve County Services," *County*, Vol. 11, No. 4, July/August 1999b.

Texas Water Development Board, "Texas Natural Resources Information System." Online at www.tnris.state.tx.us/about.htm (accessed December 2003).

Thrall, Grant I., "Demographic Ring Study Reports with GIS Technology," *Journal of Real Estate Literature*, July 1999.

U.S. Congress, "Right-to-Know After September 11th," hearing before the House Transportation and Infrastructure Committee, November 8, 2001.

U.S. Department of the Air Force, *U.S. Air Force Intelligence Targeting Guide*, Air Force Pamphlet 14-210, February 1, 1998. Online at www.e-publishing.af.mil/pubfiles/af/14/afpam14-210/afpam14-210.pdf (accessed December 2003).

U.S. Department of Commerce, National Oceanic and Atmospheric Administration, *NOAA's National Environmental Satellite, Data, and Information Service: Economic Value for the Nation*, September 2001.

U.S. Federal Geographic Data Committee, *Manual of Federal Geographic Data Products*, Hampton, Va.: ViGYAN Inc., September 1992.

U.S. Geological Survey, *The National Map: Topographic Mapping for the 21st Century*, final report, Reston, Va., November 30, 2001.

The White House, *The National Strategy for the Physical Protection of Critical Infrastructures and Key Assets*, February 2003.